What people are

Practicing Me

Practicing Mental Illness is a riveting account of the author's struggles with bipolar disorder and the incredible steps he took to manage the symptoms. By candidly sharing his story, George Hofmann takes the reader on a roller coaster ride through the extreme emotional highs and lows of the disease. Despite many setbacks, and the devastating toll it had on his personal and professional relationships, Hofmann didn't give up. He kept taking small and specific actions to move forward and ultimately change the trajectory of his life. Beautifully written, this inspirational book has the power to help so many who are suffering alone to find hope and build a life of meaning, resilience and connection during the toughest of times.
Suzie Pileggi Pawelski, MAPP, coauthor of *Happy Together: Using the Science of Positive Psychology to Build Love That Lasts*

Practicing Mental Illness is a remarkable work. A real, honest, and positively inspiring life guide. It not only helps us to better understand how various forms of mental illness truly affect us, but is a practical workbook filled with effective techniques and habits that we can use to better manage our moods, behaviors, and finally live free. As someone who has personally struggled with depression and PTSD for years, George's book is a sobering, refreshing, and hope-filled reality check that makes it clear that we not only need to accept responsibility for getting better, but put in the work. *Practicing Mental Illness* is a comforting reassurance and everyday handbook that we can use to not only be well but live a full and thriving life. I highly recommend it to anyone that has, or has a loved one struggling with, mental illness. This book can help when applied. I know this because it

has helped me.
David Pasqualone, Host, The Remarkable People Podcast

George Hofmann does a masterful job in integrating many tools for peace of mind and heart. Including mindfulness and meditation practice he dives deeply into the causes of stress and how to dissolve them. The book is filled with practical tools to apply as well as theory and discussion of many important points. I highly recommend this wonderful work.
Brenda Shoshanna, PhD, psychologist, long-term Zen practitioner, New Moon Zendo

George Hofmann has written a powerful book. Who's it for? He tells us right up front: "anyone with an affective disorder like anxiety, depression or bipolar disorder." That's an audience that is far greater than we might commonly realize. His title announces the three elements in his strategy. To meditation he adds "movement," which means doing regular exercise (even including kick-boxing and Japanese fencing) along with, no surprise, finding meaningful work.

Hofmann knows whereof he speaks. He is frank and candid in his listing of various moments of mental illness with which he has struggled, including suicide attempts. He admits to having done "reprehensible things." And he reminds us early on that "I still take my meds and probably always will." In a good first step, he recognizes that psychology can play a crucial part in one's healing. George learned with time to distinguish what he was from what he had. He had a bipolar disorder, but that disease didn't define him. He retained his sense of himself as an individual.

Another sign of Hofmann's good sense is that he labels his approach to meditation as a form of "secular mindfulness." He has a refreshingly iconoclastic view of current practice of mindfulness. This first-hand expert objects to it for, "It's too self-oriented." He condemns current practice as an "elevation of the self," which simply serves to "[reinforce] our ideal of the individual as the agent of their own well-being." That's what "predominates our culture" and may in fact "be a prime cause of suffering. Self-absorption only drowns us in more pain."

His view of meditation is far more flexible. Playing a role in that long-term commitment can be a "meditation journal." It can be used to record not just the ideas that spring up, but also one's bodily responses to those insights. Making use of such a journal, he assures us, "won't disturb the meditative process," and it can be productive "to write down [a revelatory] moment."

What Hofmann offers is a thorough introduction to some truly life-enhancing procedures and attitudes.

Jamieson Spencer, author of *Fictional Religion* and *Modified Raptures*

By the same author

Resilience: Handling Anxiety in a Time of Crisis
(Changemakers, 2020)

Practicing Mental Illness

Practices to manage challenging moods in a crazy world

Practicing
Mental Illness

Practices to manage challenging moods
in a crazy world

George Hofmann

**CHANGEMAKERS
BOOKS**

Winchester, UK
Washington, USA

JOHN HUNT PUBLISHING

First published by Changemakers Books, 2021
Changemakers Books is an imprint of John Hunt Publishing Ltd., No. 3 East Street,
Alresford, Hampshire SO24 9EE, UK
office@jhpbooks.com
www.johnhuntpublishing.com
www.changemakers-books.com

For distributor details and how to order please visit the 'Ordering' section on our website.

Text copyright: George Hofmann 2020

ISBN: 978 1 78904 626 7
978 1 78904 627 4 (ebook)
Library of Congress Control Number: 2021934894

A CIP catalogue record for this book is available from the British Library.

Design: Stuart Davies

UK: Printed and bound by CPI Group (UK) Ltd, Croydon, CR0 4YY
Printed in North America by CPI GPS partners

We operate a distinctive and ethical publishing philosophy in
all areas of our business, from our global network of authors to
production and worldwide distribution.

Contents

For Niki, without whom I would not be doing this work or enjoying this life so much. Thanks and love. And to Mom and Dad, who pulled me through the worst years and exemplified the strength needed to live well.

Acknowledgments

Thank you to everyone at Changemakers and John Hunt Publishing for bringing this work to the world, especially to publisher, editor and friend Tim Ward. For early input on the manuscript, thanks to Ronn Smith, Sherry Woods and Therese Ettel. For inspiration, ideas and lunch, a debt to Scott Vradelis. For the skepticism, John Penn and Bill Newman. All in one take to David Pasqualone, Dave Smith, Jules DeVitto and Michael Chabot for helping me work things out on the air. Thanks to Ed Breslin for the encouragement when it seemed like no one would ever see my work. To Albert Eisenberg and all at Broad + Liberty for giving me a voice. Special gratitude for Nicole and Noelle for making it very clear what works and what doesn't. And to you, my reader, I sincerely hope this helps and wish you well on your journey. Feel free to be in touch at www. practicingmentalillness.com

Introduction

The Ground Rules

Episodes of anxiety, depression or mania can crash upon you like waves. Without even seeing the storm coming, one can wind up tossed in the surf, pulled under, gasping for air. And then the waves keep coming, bringing with them the feeling that there will never be smoother water, nor any opportunity to reach the shore.

But what if there were a way to get beyond the waves and stay there? Can a person avoid the surprise of episodes that once made it so difficult to function at all? Or maybe avoid the episodes altogether? There is a way and it can apply to anyone with an affective disorder like anxiety, depression or bipolar disorder. But it involves some changes and some hard work.

The first thing that must change is the way you define yourself and your relationship with mental illness. You don't need to accept responsibility for having an illness. You will have to accept responsibility for getting better.

Then, you'll have to undertake a few practices that will be added to the medicine and therapy currently used to help manage disorder. These practices will introduce you to a new way to live with mental illness. When implemented, they can help you avoid or minimize future episodes of symptoms that were once debilitating. They may even help you avoid future episodes altogether.

To achieve this, you'll have to do the work. This book can help you map out a plan to live well despite being diagnosed with a serious mental illness. It can even lay the groundwork to help you fully recover. But the methods detailed here will only lead to success if you make the effort.

A life with a mental illness can be lived well. One with

an affective disorder can be successful, fulfilling and stable, undisturbed by serious episodes of anxiety, depression or mania. Emotions can be managed, and emotional pain can be minimized.

It's hard. Very hard. But it can be done.

And it's worth it. To live a life free of roiling moods is worth it.

* * *

My experience with mental illness resulted in two suicide attempts and six hospitalizations between the ages of 30 and 43. As is typical, I went through a few doctors and a bunch of detrimental meds before I was correctly diagnosed with mixed-episode rapid-cycling bipolar disorder 1.

Through my twenties I leapt a hypomanic vault to the top at the special-risk insurance marketer I worked for. Then I started to act impulsively and dangerously. I began to hallucinate. I went into the hospital for the first time in 1994 as a sales executive. A year later I was riddled; huddled in the stock room of a gift shop at Christmastime tying price tags onto candlesticks and place settings. I made a few dollars filing papers for an artist. It was the best I could do.

Then things got worse.

During subsequent hospitalizations doctors tried to get the meds right. I went through a long series of ECT (shock treatments). By the summer of 2002 I'd had it. I sat down in front of a coffee table that was laid out with a couple glasses of water and all the pills I had in the house. I tried to kill myself.

I was far from the promising future I had moved toward in my twenties. As I turned 40 I was working in a coffee shop and struggling to pay for my medicine. I lived with my parents. Then I decided to get better. I had a good doctor, a supportive family, and some close friends. I was lucky. I had a chance.

I had long called myself bipolar. But then I refused to continue to identify with the disease.

In my mind, bipolar disorder became an obstacle I could overcome. I still had a couple of hospitalizations in front of me before the meds were just right and the therapy yielded some positive results. But for the first time in my life I was serious about getting better and willing to do the work required to become well.

The medicine and the therapy finally worked together, and I found a place of stability. But mercurial moods still rocked this calm from time to time. I was still empty, unsatisfied, even self-loathing. In a way, managing a mental illness became as difficult as dealing with the violent storm into which bipolar disorder had pushed me. I complied with the treatment plan my doctor designed for me, but when honest with myself I had to admit that I wasn't sure it was all worth it. I judged myself harshly.

I needed something to live for. External goals and fantasies about some brighter future had failed. This something had to be found in the present and within. I looked for a reason to go on.

It seemed my entire life became a spiritual search, and in 2004 I began meditating. The practice helped me to settle down, but I assigned goals to it and found few opportunities to be present and still. Although I wasn't sure what results I sought, I wanted to get something tangible out of meditation, and get it fast. I thought I had to clear my mind and stop thinking. I thought I would be relaxed and in bliss while sitting cross-legged on a cushion. Meditation wasn't supposed to be the sometimes excruciating feelings in my body and distracting jumble of thoughts I was experiencing.

Or so I thought.

Soon the spiritual striving fell away, satisfied by the stillness I began to find. I felt less restricted by the bipolar disorder that I had so intimately related to for so long. Then I discovered that while meditating I could notice little changes in my mind and body that signaled to me an episode was coming. That gave me the opportunity to intervene and head off the worst of it. Of course my practice deepened. I slowly started to venture out of the house. I looked outside of myself to others.

I began to move around more each day. It was forced on me at first. I lived in a suburb but worked in the city. It was a long walk through town to get to the bus. Walking gave me the opportunity to meditate as well, and soon I was walking everywhere. I started to run a bit and added some stretching and calisthenics each day. I couldn't afford to join a gym, but the music and mirrors and strutting people found in a gym would have ruined the mood that movement put me in anyway.

Aside from a year spent on disability during the worst of my episodes, I have always worked. Work became a practice equal to meditation and movement. I was productive, I got paid and I made something of myself. A 44-year-old man living with his parents, I became independent. Work gave me a reason to get out of bed and an opportunity to give back and help others in a way others had helped me.

I began to work at an agency with programs for people with developmental disabilities and brain injuries. The work was meaningful, and I thrived. I even became well enough to meet someone special, get married and have a child.

That's where I find myself today—a living testament to the benefits of meditation, movement and meaningful work. Life has become a practice focused on these three things, and because of that practice I'm able to stay well, contribute, love and learn.

I haven't been hospitalized since I started meditating. I haven't even had any significant episodes of mania or depression. Because of exercise I haven't developed even one of the many life-threatening physical diseases so often comorbid with bipolar disorder. Work helps me stay engaged, touch others and remain independent.

Putting it all together was the most challenging thing I've ever done. It's easy to give up and be sick. It takes so much effort to be well. But that effort is the best work of all, and for years it has helped me keep the worst of mental illness, the symptoms and the suffering and the dependency, at bay.

I'm different than I used to be. I whisper it, because although it's been years, I admit it still feels a bit odd: I think I'm doing pretty well.

The Ground Rules

Ground rule 1: Don't say, "I am mentally ill"

Before practicing therapies to get over a mental illness, some ground rules must be set. The first involves your relationship with your disease. How do you relate to your mental illness, and how do you describe yourself?

Language can have a powerful influence over self-definition, revelation and healing. The way we describe ourselves and our condition speaks volumes about our outlook and our outcomes. I was diagnosed decades ago with bipolar disorder, I still adhere to treatment, and I still suffer occasional disruptive mood changes. Yet I strongly maintain that I am not bipolar.

For years I agreed with doctors and other healing professionals and I used the phrase, "I am mentally ill." After all, I had all the symptoms: I was psychotic, I was terribly socially inhibited, I destroyed relationships and finances during manic episodes, and eventually, after much trial and error, I responded to treatment. Diagnosis correct, hence, "I am bipolar."

But that phrase always bothered me.

Place an object after a noun and the verb "to be" and the result is identity. I'm comfortable with the fact that I am a man, I am 57 years old, and I am short. But maintaining that I am a disease always struck me as damaging.

How can I recover from a condition, how can I lose it, if I am it?

It struck me that bipolar is not who I am, but instead something I have. You see, no one says I am hypertension or I am cancer. Why not? Because that's not who they are. The diseases are something they have. What damage was I doing to myself by identifying with the idea that I am bipolar?

So I changed the language I used to describe myself. I maintained not that "I am mentally ill," but instead that "I have a mental illness." It caused a sea change in my treatment and my recovery. Suddenly I was not a damaged person. I simply had a medical condition like any other, and it could be treated and I could manage it. Maybe I could even remove its influence from my life.

No longer would I allow anyone, not doctors, not family, not anyone, to say that I was bipolar. I insisted on, "You have bipolar disorder." I'm not splitting hairs here. The difference is huge, and I encourage you to adopt this language in describing yourself and your own condition. I can guarantee that you will change your relationship to the challenges that mental illness brings to your life.

If you are something, well, that's who you are. If you have something, you can get over it, or minimize it, or manage it. You can stand apart from it. You alone are complete. The things you have are influential, yes, but malleable. I believe that if we insist on the verbiage that we have a mental illness, instead of that we are mentally ill, we can focus more on positive treatment and even defeat the stigma surrounding our challenges.

It concerns me that today I see young people who have been diagnosed with bipolar disorder or other affective disorders identify with the disease and fully incorporate it into their self-image.

Yes, it is necessary to accept the disorder and yes, it is true that beneficial things can come of one's experience with mental illness. But we must consider our impact on others in our lives. All mental illness remains challenging to others. Society demands some basic behaviors from each of us, and we must be able to be independent and self-supporting. If identifying with a disease prevents that, the identity should be questioned.

Again, I think it's beneficial to say you have a mental illness. All the learning and love can still follow. You just won't limit yourself by succumbing to the self-definition that you are ill, or dangerously different, or damaged in any way.

The language we use can shine a tremendous light on who we think we are. And who we think we are is a full, productive, and healing, compassionate person, and that person is independent of the things doctors tell us we have. I can comfortably say, "I have bipolar disorder."

Only by standing apart from this affective disorder was I able to imagine living without its pervasive impact on my actions. I had to establish an identity that did not include bipolar disorder or its symptoms. Sure I still have it, but it's not who I am.

The same goes for depression and anxiety. They can wreak havoc on a person's life, but they are not the person.

In applying practices in focused attention to treat an illness, you will find that the practice enables you to observe the illness as it acts on you. You will also see that if your self-definition is caught up in a disease, the self-definition is limited and incorrect. Only then can you change. Only then can it go away.

So, ground rule number one is: Don't say, "I am mentally ill." Instead say, "I have a mental illness."

Ground rule 2: Keep taking your meds and keep seeing your doctor and/or therapist

I maintain, and insist, that meditation, movement and meaningful work are adjunct therapies. I believe they are absolutely necessary to manage mental illness, so in this sense one may think of them as primary. I just don't want to imply that they will replace medication and psychotherapy.

Medication and psychotherapy have the proof of years of research and practice to illustrate their efficacy. Using these therapies, 85% of people with bipolar disorder's conditions will improve. Therapy will make over 70% of those with anxiety or depression better. But 64% of people with mental illness will stop taking their meds as directed at some point in their treatment, and months or years of talk therapy become very expensive and the number of sessions is often limited by health insurance plans. If these treatments work so well, why do so many people, knowing they'll likely get sick again, stop them?

Possibly because these people overidentify with their mental illness and to get well feels uncomfortable, and possibly because, even when medically treated well, life still sucks.

Sure, side effects and cost factor into many people's decision to stop taking meds or stop seeing their therapist, but these can be addressed by conscientious doctors and therapists. As side effects go, many drugs are available for various mental illnesses, so if a person is treatment resistant to one, or the drug has too many unpleasant side effects, another is surely available to try. (Some people are truly treatment resistant to many, if not all, medications. If you're one of them my heart goes out to you. But read on. There are still therapies that can help.)

As for cost, only 9% of the people taking medication for mental illness are on brand-name medication. The rest of us take generics which are much less expensive. Even if the generics cost too much, programs exist that will help those with the lowest incomes afford their meds. And Medicaid and most private health insurance plans cover all generics.

Although medication and talk therapy can make all the worst symptoms of a mental illness go away, life may still be disappointing. This is a terrible letdown that's hard for many people to overcome. Many will deal with the side effects and the cost and the sacrifice and still find life unsatisfying. It happened to me. I felt better but I still suffered.

There was a summer when it seemed everything was going well for everyone I knew. But I was still sick. The worst of my bipolar disorder was controlled, but I couldn't stick to a sensible routine and stay healthy. Physically I was OK. Yet things still seemed wrong. At the time I was taking an anti-convulsant that made me gain weight and an antipsychotic that wiped me out. I also had a PRN, a "take as needed," for an anti-anxiety med.

My doctor was a Canadian working in the USA. His visa status was changing, so he couldn't practice for a few months. I didn't want to start over with someone new, so I just quit. I didn't show up for talk therapy, and within a few weeks I stopped taking my meds, except for the anti-anxiety pill, a controlled substance, which I began to abuse.

It didn't end well.

I spun out of control, cycling between psychotic mania and suicidal depression. I cut myself habitually and drank tequila like it was water. I crushed the anti-anxiety pills and snorted them. Then I attempted suicide.

After a long hospitalization I emerged on meds that didn't feel quite as bad when I took them as the meds I took before the suicide attempt, and my doctor returned and we began therapy again. My moods leveled and I became more patient with the slow progress I was making. I just got by, but I was getting by.

When I added meditation, a practice in focused attention, to the mix of meds and talk, life brightened. Moods stopped slamming me and I stopped identifying with the disease. While I don't want to wean you off your meds, I don't want to imply that you have to wait until everything is well to begin the therapies detailed in this book, either. Practices in disciplined focused attention complement medicine and talk therapy, and they are meant to be undertaken together.

While I believe these therapies of meditation, movement and meaningful work are crucial to live well, I must again insist that to overcome mental illness, medication and psychotherapy remain primary, especially soon after a diagnosis of mental illness strikes someone down. It would be irresponsible for me to even hint that if you meditate or exercise enough you can get off your meds. Sure, there may be anecdotal evidence that people have done this, but much science weighs on the benefits of medication and talk. I'm not about to stand up to science and say I know better.

I do know what made life better for me after the meds kicked in and the talk was underway and I began to move toward stability: practices in focused attention.

After many years of talk with my doctor we don't undertake psychotherapy much anymore. My doctor and I uncovered and dealt with some pretty big stuff, and he's still available if I need to work on specific issues. It is important that I have this "on-call" arrangement with him. Many people who delve into a meditation practice uncover some uncomfortable, even painful revelations about their own suffering. In many cultures, meditation was developed specifically to address suffering, and it is very good at that. Still, no one should suffer alone. In fact, you shouldn't think of meditation as something you do alone. It's best practiced in a community. As you begin to meditate, or return to meditation, or continue with meditation, it is important to have a means to address the painful issues that may come up while you practice. For many of us, living on our own with an individual practice, this is a relationship with a good therapist. In deep therapy community can be formed. Bring friends and loved ones into this honest circle and a community enlarges and becomes complete. Church or support groups are other good options.

I still take my meds and probably always will. I have too much at risk to stop them, and my doctor thinks coming off of them could be catastrophic. Even so, it's the adjunct therapies that make life worth living, and along with the medication and psychotherapy these practices help level things. If I wasn't practicing the therapies noted in this book I'd have no love, hell, I'd have no life, at all. I'd feel no love for myself, and certainly no love for or maybe even from anyone else.

It takes a lot of work and discipline. Anything worth it does. If you want to begin, first listen to your doctor. Take your meds and seek professional talk therapy when you need to. Then begin to practice meditation, move around, and find something to put some effort into that helps you focus, learn and feel a sense of accomplishment.

Meditation, movement and meaningful work, when combined with medication and psychotherapy, are likely to minimize the most intransigent defeats of an affective disorder. All you have to do is bring some practiced focus into your life. Not a focus on something you want to be, but a focus on what is happening right now. The good and the bad. Then you can see things as they are and act to change things for the better.

Ground rule 3: Exercise self-discipline, but keep it gentle

Much of what I recommend as a path toward wellness involves great self-discipline and some self-sacrifice. But I realized early in my practice that if the discipline and sacrifice were too severe, my efforts would border on ascetic austerity. That's not necessary.

Some things make sense. Meditating at the same time every day establishes it as a healthy habit. I get up early, before my wife and daughter, and put in a half-hour on the cushion. Exercise is scheduled, too, with some calisthenics early in the day and a good walk later. As for work, it is important to show up every day and resist the temptation to call in sick when moods get rocky or anxiety threatens to trap me inside the house. When I work from home I need to avoid the TV and the deep rabbit hole of social media and the internet.

My life is a bit less spontaneous than it was when mania fueled my more exuberant years, but sticking to a schedule allows for treasured moments of exciting experiences with less trouble attached. When the schedule is broken by will and whims, I know an episode is brewing. Then I can act and keep it from disrupting my life and the responsibilities I must fulfill.

I've lived my life embracing libertarian, even anarchistic philosophy. Oddly, my proclivity to follow Benedictine and Zen monastic practices may expose me as one secretly seeking rules. I set out to counter a life of excess and for a while fell for the opposite extreme. Asceticism became an overt form of expression and I overdid it. At least I became less attached to things and was able to resist the temptation to spend while manic.

As austere practices made life simpler, my life became complicated by hyper-religiosity. I went to mass every day. I spent a retreat at a Zen monastery where during meditation sessions a monitor stalked the hall carrying a stick that looked like a canoe paddle. If anyone slouched in their posture or nodded off, the monitor would whack them on the shoulder. And I was liking this stuff!

The primary-source ancient texts about meditation that I studied advocate a middle way, and I needed to find mine. It landed between the excesses of brewing mania and the self-denial of deep depression. I had to stop regimenting my life so strictly, for there was no room for creative expression. But I had to organize it and establish a sensible routine. In seeking to be gentler with myself, I thought about discipline and how my wife and I approach it with our daughter.

When a parent disciplines a child, it is at best an act of love; not an act to unreasonably restrict behavior or creativity, and not an act to helicopter over every possible outcome. The parent seeks to establish parameters within which the child can make their own decisions. When emotions result in tantrums, the parent uses discipline to help the child pull themselves together and return to some sense of self-control. Discipline is necessary to help the child grow and, when the opportunity presents itself, to make good decisions. When the child makes a poor choice, the child must encounter the natural consequences of that choice. Given the parent's instruction and example, combined with reasonable discipline, the child's choices will be based on moral fairness and positive consideration.

I had to view self-discipline the same way.

Only when I stopped trying to beat the shifting moods out of myself through severe restrictions on my behavior could I avoid being grumpy, intolerant and boring. I hold to a routine but find varied experiences within that routine. I don't limit my freedom without reason, and I find freedom within limits. I know one can color within the lines and still make some beautiful, creative art.

Moods are a natural expression of emotions and are healthy when skillfully expressed. If moods rage out of control or lead a person to do unreasonable things, some healthy self-discipline can restore the turbulent mind to composure. If one applies discipline and sacrifice to ever so slightly shave off the highs and the lows, and lives without the most impulsive behavior, one can achieve a life of consistent rewards. A person can stay present enough to be fair to, and available for, those who care for them, and those who need care.

Down the path of reasoned self-discipline the meaning of life can be found.

Ground rule 4: You must take responsibility for all your actions

When I asked you to not define yourself as mentally ill (ground rule 1), I stated that while you're exempt from responsibility for being ill, you need to take responsibility for getting better. Ground rule 4 expands on that.

I remember when I was dating my wife. The night I told her I have bipolar disorder, she touched me deeply when she asked what could she do to help if I had a difficult period. I returned that kindness by vowing to never use my illness as an excuse for bad behavior.

Now I've done some pretty reprehensible things in the past, especially while manic. It would be easy to excuse these faults of conscience as prompted by an episode and performed completely outside of my control. There have been times when I was irrational, psychotic even. It is easy to blame some of the worst things I've done, like cheating in relationships, abusing drugs and alcohol, or diving deep into debt, let alone trying to kill myself, on this lack of reason and bipolar-fueled delusion and irresponsibility. I may not have even been aware of what I was doing at the time.

Forget about matters of blame. The idea is to not get hung up on excuses. Accept myself? Yes. But accept, too, the things I have done.

No matter how much a fault in judgment can be explained as an act committed without thought during an episode of my disorder, I still have to own the consequences. I still have to take responsibility for all I've done, make what amends I can, ask sincerely to be forgiven, and strive to be ethical, compassionate, and forward looking in my actions. I ask you to take the same responsibility for your actions, no matter the cause. Then, as best you can, make the situation better.

Forgiveness and the opportunity to make restitution are earned and important. We must learn from our failings and do whatever we can to not repeat them. Mental illness can strongly influence our behavior and interfere with our ability to choose well. But we do choose. We must try to choose best. We must live with, and rectify, all the bad we do—to ourselves and to others.

Most of the practices I detail in this book involve being fully in the moment, experiencing the present, and relinquishing the pull of thoughts that take us away from our current experience. However, this must not be seen as a method to release awareness of or responsibility for what we have done in the past, even as we seek to not get hung up reliving our mistakes. Also, a present-moment focus does not relieve us of planning for a responsible and independent future.

There is a moral component to this. We do not want to be a burden to others, yet we can't get to good health entirely on our own. We rely on so many people and programs to help us recover and heal. We have a duty to take responsibility for what we do and how we heal as a means to thank those who help us and to pay them back. We must reveal ourselves as worthy of their assistance.

I believe there is a moral law of cause and effect at work in the world, and a lot of that cause and effect concerns how we treat other people. Society is moving toward a great emphasis on rights for all sorts of groups of people, including those of us with mental illness. We must never abdicate our responsibility for society or ignore the consequences of our actions as we demand these rights. What matters most as we advocate for and develop ourselves is how we treat others. Even if we misstep under the influence of the worst episodes of our disorders.

So take responsibility for your actions. Always.

Ground rule 5: Stay open to new ideas; don't think you know it all

This one was the hardest one for me to adopt.

I've always been very curious, so the new ideas part wasn't too difficult. In fact, sometimes my experience with mental illness made me very vulnerable to influences I might not have chosen on a better day. While I ramped up into a manic episode I'd adopt some new persona or fall into an interest or belief and go way overboard as I expressed my new lifestyle. This has happened with things as varied as objectivism, liberation theology, and fly-fishing. I'd go full into something to the exclusion of all else, only to drop it entirely as I settled down and recovered.

Oddly enough, all of these new personas were self-generated. I ignored teachers and didn't fall under the influence of others, other than what I read in books. For the things I'm truly serious about, like history or economics, my knowledge would have come along so much more complete and reasoned if I had sought a teacher early on. Instead, I thought I'd figure it all out myself. Of course, I was always right. Even when I was wrong. I was an insufferable know-it-all.

Ideas I had would get knocked down and contradicted, but I held my ground. Sometimes I was right, after all. But often I held on to erroneous thoughts for way too long. Especially erroneous thoughts and judgments about myself. That's no way to heal.

We benefit the most when we share with others, and nowhere is this more true than with ideas. So many people have had shared experiences, and so many others have in the past been where you find yourself now. Learn from them. There's always someone who knows more about a topic than you do who is worth listening to. Diverse opinions, those very different from yours, will either help you shore up your beliefs or clue you in to where you are wrong. The most admirable intellects, the successful people most worthy of esteem, are open and flexible.

While I encourage you to supplement your knowledge with words and examples from varied teachers, I don't contradict myself by saying you should question everything they tell you. No one learns without inquiry. Learning is key to growing, so don't take anything at face value, and don't take anything for granted. When you are absolutely sure you know everything about something, or if you're under the influence of someone who acts like they do, it's time to enter some doubt. Ask tough questions about the things you're most sure of.

We live in a world where it's too easy to just reinforce your own beliefs and never give serious consideration to opposing views. If you're so sure about everything, you'll never learn anything new. Remember, with little doubt comes little knowledge—with great doubt comes great knowledge.

I'm going to offer a lot of ideas to manage mental illness in the next few chapters. But don't take my word for it. Try the practices and see how they work for you. You're going to have to execute them with attention if you're going to find out if they help. There's a lot of advice in this book. Take the advice that resonates with, and works for, you. But try it all out, even if you're sure it won't work. You might be surprised.

Be curious and never think you know it all. You never know who you might learn from.

* * *

So, ground rules established, it's time to move into the therapies that produce wellness. But how will all this help?

Meditation can help a person become less attached to an illness and the troubles it causes. You can notice the inaccuracy of your thoughts, and experience things in a fresh way that will help you reframe your views of yourself and the world. You can realize how thoughts about events and emotions can make you suffer more than the events and emotions themselves. You can get beyond the prison of exceptional, but familiar, pain. Meditation can even give birth to self-awareness mature enough to help you predict when your mood is about to change, and to intervene and avoid the worst disruptions your mental illness can present.

Movement will make you feel better all around. In lives ravaged by mental illness much seems out of our control. But physical fitness is one of the things we can control. We can always get into better shape and be healthier. We can always regain a sense of accomplishment along the way. Old clichés like "strong body, strong mind" stick with us because they're true. And to be physically fit can help us deal with some of the nasty side effects of the medicine we must take. Plus, it will help us sleep better and act with more vitality. Maybe most important, movement will help us avoid many of the diseases like heart disease, high blood pressure and diabetes that are comorbid with many mental illnesses, and that cut many lives short.

Meaningful work may be the most important kick in the pants of all. While many people say we should not be defined by our work anymore than we should be defined by our illness, work can give us a reason to push on when all else fails. To lie on the couch and accomplish nothing will only reinforce the belief that mental illness makes us worthless. To get up and do something; to be productive; to contribute to our well-being and our futures; to serve others through our efforts; these things can complete a journey into wellness. Of course, the best reasons to go on will be found within us, but the chief way of expressing those reasons is through effort, accomplishment and service. No work is insignificant if it helps us heal. The work we put into ourselves is as important as the work that produces good for others. Productivity can help us get in touch with the best of ourselves.

It's time to begin. We'll start with meditation. I hope you find out right away that it's not what you think it is.

Section One

Meditation

The mind is its own place, and in itself
Can make a heav'n of hell, a hell of heav'n.
—John Milton, *Paradise Lost*, 1667

Chapter One

Focused Attention

Using the word "meditation" and expecting a consensus is like using the word "exercise" and expecting people to identify common physical practices. The word can mean so many different things, and everyone has their own idea about what it is and how to do it. And let's not even bring up the word "mindfulness," which is so trendy and overused today that it has nearly been shorn of all meaning.

Meditative practices exist in all cultures and are described in some of humanity's earliest literature. As practices appeared around the world they emerged with some key similarities. Meditation has always involved some sort of focused attention and an intense awareness of present experience. Much can be gained by placing your focus on the breath or a mantra or an object, as most traditions recommend. In fact, the method of practice, the how to do it, is strikingly similar across cultures. Whatever you seek from meditation, whatever you're trying to accomplish, whether it's full immersion in the moment or simple stress relief, the actual practice is often the same.

I came to meditation during a period of hyper-religiosity during a manic episode. Bad beginning, but it stuck. I performed the Divine Office as practiced by monks in the Benedictine tradition of the Catholic Church. It involves a recitation of certain psalms at certain times of day. The focus is on the repeated words and the deep spiritual impulse. The idea is to clear the mind of all else and achieve a direct experience of God in this moment. I did this because psychosis drove me to think the survival of good in the world depended on my doing it.

I never did meet God. I deepened the practice as mania continued to bubble up in me and I filled with religious imagery.

Of course I overdid it. I locked myself in my apartment at all hours and took a little pocket-sized book of the Psalms with me on the bus and to work so I wouldn't miss a matins, lauds, vespers or compline (all names for different times of day when the Psalms are chanted). I even inquired at some monasteries about becoming a monk, but the entry requirements mandated by the few abbots I contacted informed me I was too old to release any attachment to worldly pleasures. I would not succeed as a monk.

I read a lot and came across Thomas Merton and Elaine MacInnes. They wrote/write from the point of view of two deeply devout Catholics who discovered, and practiced, Zen meditation. They remained Catholic. Zen meditation seemed deceptively simple, and soon I retired the Psalms and spent my time meditating just sitting, staring at a wall, my focus on the breath, per the instructions of Zen teachers.

I was first assaulted by the harsh reality of my thoughts. Then, when I got past the sense that I had been overdoing it as an urban monk ghosting through the material world, I discovered that most of my thoughts had no relationship to reality at all. Even as I became sane again. My mind was ablaze, filled with plans and fears and doubts and worries and expectations and all sorts of stuff that distracted me from what I was actually experiencing right here right now. My mind had something to say about everything. Usually it was wrong.

Lost in a spin of fantasy and clutching to some poor idea of myself that didn't hold up to inspection, I missed a lot of the little things that make up a life. Little things like the fact that I was going crazy again. I used meditation as some path to become enlightened, even though I had no idea what that meant. I tried it all: contemplative prayer, lovingkindness, mantra chanting, but I kept coming back to simple Zen practice. Just sitting there, breathing, asking questions and noticing stuff.

It was the noticing that finally helped.

Before I could notice anything, though, I had to deal with the grandiosity that came with the mania that clung to me. I thought I could be a Zen master, and spent time at a Zen monastery where I was held back by ideas of my own instead of opening up to silence. I was afraid to admit to ignorance and would not concede to an authority, not even a person with lineage. I wouldn't actually learn anything. Oddly, while I honestly sought answers, I felt above it all.

The Zen monasteries made me feel a little silly, too. People put on robes and rang bells and chanted in Asian languages. It seemed an awful lot like the Catholic mass that I knew so well, albeit with different chants. Similar performance, different message. But a message cloaked in ritual took flight in my mind. I missed the entire point of emptiness and doubt that Zen exposes.

Then the whole mindfulness thing took off. Everybody was paying attention (actually almost no one was paying attention, that's the whole point of what went wrong). Companies were holding workshops for their employees on stress relief and creativity using the same meditation techniques I thought I had mastered. So I began to teach. I did a few corporate presentations, workshops at yoga studios and wellness centers, and a drop-in meditation series at a church.

I picked up some credentials in Mindfulness-Based Stress Reduction (MBSR), or Management, depending on who branded it. I studied in a practicum at the Penn Program for Mindfulness, and spent an intense retreat studying with the founders of MBSR, Jon Kabat Zinn and Saki Santorelli. But I was just jumping on a bandwagon that soon claimed cures for everything from anxiety to blood sugar levels, the entire movement peppered by money-hungry underqualified self-proclaimed experts who began to overpromise results for too little effort. The founders were onto something. But the followers took it way too far.

Suddenly there were mindfulness magazines and mindfulness

apps, and fancy, expensive mindfulness meditation furniture, bells and timers. I retreated from the whole charade and went back to my room and sat on my cushion and put in a lot of work just meditating.

I think that's when I finally became serious about practice. Instead of projecting myself onto some big world of guruness, I became quiet and sat, just breathing, paying attention to what I was feeling and the walls of thought my mind ran into as I tried to sit still. Instead of counting achievements I counted breaths, and soon my moods leveled out and I became more stable. I could tell things were changing and I could act to make those changes positive. Most of the time.

Meditation gave me a way to finally manage my bipolar disorder.

I realized I didn't know anything about enlightenment, and I had no clue about the answers to big questions. Hell, when I completed a self-report survey assessment of mindfulness, I came out not very mindful at all. But when it came to meditation and mental illness, I was making progress.

It had to do with just sitting there, noticing things.

Attention and Awareness

There are a few technical things about attention and awareness we have to address. The words are not interchangeable. Awareness is where the mind and body unified finds itself in all it perceives. Five senses collect information about our environment and all that is in it, as well as all the feelings that are in us, and return that information as our reality. Then we add thoughts to the mix. If I'm sitting on my patio reading a book and petting the dogs, everything around me and in me makes up my field of awareness.

The chair I sit on, the warmth of the sun, the birds singing in the tree beyond the wall, the book I've lost my place in because some thought about a siren blowing by distracted me; all of this and so much more construct my awareness.

But that's not all. There is another world inside of me that competes with the world around me. There's the slight pain in my shoulder from how I slept last night, the nagging voice that says I should be inside cleaning the kitchen, the impression of the words in the book as I read them, what I think about the words I'm reading, and all the other thoughts that come up that wipe out any comprehension of the last sentence, and make me lose the bird song, forget the pain in my shoulder, and obliterate all the sensory information I'm receiving.

An awful lot is going on at any one time. It's hard to keep up with it or blot it out even if we want to. Just when we comprehend it all, some random thought or outside distraction will jump up and pull us away from all of it.

In all this jumble of thoughts and stimulation, or boredom, there's often one thing that takes us, if only for a fleeting moment. Something stands out and pulls us in. Maybe it's the birdsong, or a dog's bark, or a word in the book we have to look up. That's what we attend to. In fact, each thing we perceive as we exist in awareness, thoughts and focus jumping all over the place, is attention.

Attention can be a choice. It is if we particularly stay with one thing. It's usually not a choice, though, as we constantly survey our world taking in volumes of information in every instant, only to have all of it wiped out by some unrelated thought or feeling that takes us out of what's happening around and within us. That focus jumping around from one thing to another? That's attention.

Attention exists within awareness. As it bounces from thoughts to feelings, we can grab it and place it somewhere within that awareness; on a sound, or an idea, or something nagging in our body, anything really, and hold it there. That's focused attention. Trouble is, we're unlikely to hold the attention where we choose to for long before it scampers off again against our will to something else. But we can try to maintain a focus on one thing. That's meditation.

Exercises in focused attention, meditation practices, involve grabbing the attention and placing it on something on purpose. Of course, distractions will always pull the attention away to something else. Something specific, something painful or pleasant, or some wash of reverie that can make us forget even where we are or that time has passed. But we can wrestle with the attention and bring it back to our point of focus. Over and over again.

A lot of things can be used to anchor the attention while meditating. I use the breath as I inhale and exhale. Some use a word or a string of words or sounds, comprehensible or not, called a mantra. Pictures or icons are used. Introduced sounds, feelings in the body, anything that remains stable and constant while we try to hold our attention on it will suffice. The only limit to the focus of attention is that it shouldn't be something that makes you think even more than you normally would when you're still. You want to avoid starting a conversation with yourself. Big questions, like what is the meaning of life, are fun to sit and ponder, but a wandering mind, an intellectual puzzle, or brainstorming ideas are not very effective for this sort of focused attention. The goal is to open yourself up to thoughts and sensations in the body and experience them, not to purposefully prompt them or try to figure them out as they come. There's plenty of time for that when you're not meditating.

It should be noted that meditation is not about not thinking. You're unlikely to clear your mind completely no matter how hard you focus on one thing. Too many people think they're failures at meditation because their mind never settles and thoughts never stop. But the mind can't operate without always thinking, and it won't for long. Then there's the body, always handing off aches and pains, or pleasures. Anyone who takes up any practice in focused attention is soon shocked by how distracted they always are.

So if you don't sit there and totally cleanse your mind, then what's the point? Why meditate at all?

Practicing meditation, or any focused attention exercise, is an enormous step into the present. We live from the shoulders up, so often lost in our heads that we completely miss what is going on within and around us. Our poor bodies suffer ignored and we rarely notice much about the places in which we exist.

When we start to focus, we start to notice things.

Observing and Discovering

I spent years wandering around preoccupied with ideas. Nothing wrong with that, but I missed so much. My life was full of fantasy and it seemed I always wanted to be somewhere other than where I was. Such fantasy is the root of play, and not always a bad thing. But with my thoughts elsewhere I ignored a relationship and felt dissatisfied with my job. This was troubling because no situation I was in was a particularly bad one. They were all pretty good, in fact. I just wasn't paying attention. I screwed up, imagined it all gone, and got exactly what I wished for.

But I didn't truly know what I wanted. It turned out my relationship was fine and my job was great and both were now gone. Mental illness fueled this dissatisfaction, yes, but I could have been more focused, nonetheless. Always placing myself in some faraway fantasy guaranteed only that I would never be satisfied. Yes, there's always room to improve oneself and one's situation, but that doesn't have to mean throwing it all away every time one's mood changes. Incremental change can inspire awe. Lots of difficult situations just need a little adjustment. But this requires an awful lot of focus and a little less judgment. Without that, I just never noticed how good I had it.

I didn't notice myself getting sick, either. I raced into mania spending money, having affairs, polluting my body with drugs and drink, and I completely missed that things were changing. Maybe I could have gotten help sooner, before I really screwed up and wanted to die, if only I'd noticed. But I wasn't tuned in. I wasn't focused on anything, let alone a simple breath during a period of meditation. That numbness I felt? That was life passing me by.

When I started to meditate I began to notice things. There were amazing feelings in my body, and when my thoughts congealed, I had a few good ones. I noticed what people around me needed, and I began to understand what motivated, challenged and bothered me. The sky was bluer than I'd imagined, food tasted better, people were more interesting. And the days no longer flew by in a blur.

But then I noticed some things that bothered me while I meditated. Yes, it seemed like I was having a good, often relaxing experience, but my thoughts betrayed some deeper trouble. The stress relief and calming period of 30 minutes on the cushion were real, but they were superficial. Finally I followed the instructions of a teacher. I sat with good posture. I focused my attention on my breath. When thoughts pulled my attention away, I let the thoughts go without completing them or beginning an internal dialogue. I placed my attention right back on my breath. This happened over and over again. It seemed meditation was an exercise in failure. I tried to keep my attention focused, but intruding thoughts or random feelings in my body constantly pulled me away.

I practiced for a few weeks and it got worse.

At first the thoughts were just a jumble, just white noise of rapid-fire distractions. But then they became separate, distinct, and overwhelming. I didn't know it at the time, but I was doing it right. I didn't know that since the thoughts came one at a time and clearer, I was focusing well and taking steps toward true attention. I just felt like I did with so many other things. I tried. I put so much work into this and it didn't work. I was failing again. I didn't realize that was the point.

I learned to count breaths. I counted as I exhaled from one up to ten. I repeated it again and again. If I lost my place, I just returned to one and started over. I never seemed to make it to ten and stop, I was so distracted. Then a teacher told me to label each thought. That would make them both concrete and complete. Naming the thought what it was made it less likely that I would be compelled to add to it. It helped me seal the thought and let it pass, enabling me to bring my attention back to my breath.

What kind of labels did I use? Well, if I was sitting there thinking about what I was going to cook for dinner, I labeled that a "plan." If I thought of a time I treated someone badly, that became a "regret." A thought about my daughter getting a role in a play was a "hope," and stewing over a bill too large to pay with this paycheck was a "worry." Every thought had a category it fell into that I could label. I noticed some patterns.

There were a lot of fantasies. There always have been. They were escapist when I used to meditate at the top of the stairs to my apartment, staring down into the dark stairwell. Today I meditate in a very nice room. I sit on a comfortable cushion surrounded by my books, my true inspirations. One or both of our dogs often curls up beside me. The sun streams through the windows and the sounds of the city gently assert themselves outside.

And still, all too often I imagine myself someplace else.

So many fantasies of things to do, places to go, people to meet fill my mind. I seem incapable of being satisfied with what I have and where I am. I'm not saying growth is a bad thing. Change can be a good goal if it's well-reasoned. But I always want more of everything, and those thoughts make it pretty difficult to stay present and experience what's going on right now, especially if something else, somewhere else, seems so much better.

Yet I don't know what all that would truly be like. I know we need to be careful what we wish for, because when we think something new will make everything better for us, we're often wrong. And if we get it, when it disappoints, it's hard to recover. Especially when it screws up all the good things we have right now. But mood changes seldom give a person room to stop and consider their actions.

I notice these thoughts, label them reverie and fantasy, and try to put them away. Most of the time, for me, today is really OK. Unless I think it isn't.

A lot of the thoughts I first noticed were very judgmental. With some of them I judged others for things they did to hurt me or someone I love. But most of the judgment was reserved for myself, and it was harsh. I discovered that much of the day I beat myself up for things I did to, or ways I affected, others. I made a ton of mistakes. Some I could rectify and some I couldn't. In ruminating on them, I treated myself pretty badly, even long after those mistakes were forgotten or forgiven by everyone else.

Then I noticed something. Many of these self-judgments were undeserved. If I'd acted without malice or played little role in an undesirable outcome, why judge myself as the villain? I'd get angry at myself, or someone else, about something that happened some time ago only to admit in a quiet moment that each of us had little to do with things going wrong. There doesn't always have to be someone to blame. Some things are out of our control. Sometimes bad things happen without anyone being at fault.

In 2002 I tried to kill myself. I took a few handfuls of pills and crawled into bed and aspirated. My mother found me the next morning and my father sat with me in the recovery room, desperate. He and I were very close, and my suicide attempt affected him deeply. He judged himself responsible for it and blamed himself. Only he had nothing to do with it. My illness and my outcome were not his fault at all. But he didn't see it that way.

Then he got sick. Very sick.

Quickly the self-judgment fell to me. I read that following a suicide attempt someone very close to the attempter often gets very ill. The stress of the event does them in. My father suffered from an auto-immune neuropathy and nearly died. I blamed myself. For years. It came up all the time while I meditated, the judgment of myself as responsible for my father's illness, and I couldn't forgive myself or shake the responsibility that, after all, wasn't really mine.

The judgment at first held back our healing. We were each so full of self-blame for the other's trouble that it was impossible to reach out and understand the other's suffering. We couldn't help ourselves and we couldn't help each other. We each broke under the burden of self-judgment and finally mustered the strength to reach out to each other. My contemplation shifted. Instead of obsessing on all the things I did wrong, I considered ways I could help things get better. We each assumed the posture that we would not get better until we brought the other one along with us. We saw the judgment of ourselves as false, and instead we found ways to ameliorate each other's pain. We both recovered and healed.

I wasn't done with the suicide attempt, however. Although I released myself from responsibility for my father's illness, forgiving myself for trying to kill myself was another thing entirely. I felt compelled to reach out for forgiveness from all the people I hurt that night I tried to extinguish my own suffering and caused so much suffering for everyone else. Guilt and anger peppered my meditation sessions.

It was when I was on a long meditation retreat in 2013, 11 years after the attempt, that it all came crashing down on me. I felt all the grief I caused and, in my mind, touched all the people I hurt. I cried for hours. Then I came home, related my story, and found that no one had really considered my suicide attempt for a very long time. They'd all dealt with it long ago and thought the whole notion of my begging for forgiveness for it silly. They were over it. Turns out the horror of my past was all in my head. I dragged it into the present and anchored myself to it to screw up my future. The event did happen, but its repercussions were a thought construct. I finally learned to let it go.

Letting go of such a big, existential issue helped me when I returned to the more mundane, nagging thoughts that interrupt my focus when I meditate today. Plans and dreams and worries and fears, and judgments, all come up every time I sit and focus on my breath. I'm able to watch each thought, each holding a label, drift off like a bubble and burst. As the imaginary mist from the pierced bubble rains on my face, I return my attention to the breath, to the present, and go on until the timer chimes. I continue with full attention into the life of the day, more stable and more centered, even if challenged by difficult things that come up during practice.

You Can't Make It All Go Away

It's easy for meditation teachers to say, "Notice your thoughts and let them go." It becomes almost a cliché when we ask you to do this non-judgmentally. I realize that, at times, some things are too big to just let go of. A sick child or a lost job are nearly impossible to label and watch drift off unconsidered. You just can't, and probably you shouldn't. But you're meditating for a fixed period of time that will soon end. Experience will show you that focused attention can make you more vital and creative, maybe even more compassionate. When presented with a huge, pressing concern, don't try to force it away. Allow yourself to just put it down for a moment. Imagine yourself grabbing the problem, holding it gently, and placing it on the floor beside you. Set it down and continue meditating. Oh, it will still be there when you're finished, but you're likely to be better prepared to deal with it.

Also, sometimes when meditating some pretty big realization will come up and you'll be terrified of losing it. Give yourself permission to stop everything and write a profound, groundbreaking thought down. Meditation is not for brainstorming to solve a tangible problem, it's for focus on the present to overcome distractions. Yet it's for noticing things, too. You don't want to lose a really good big idea, or a breakthrough in something you've been working on. Write it down. When the idea is committed to paper, saved and safe, forget it and get back to your point of focus and your dismissal of random thoughts that strain and pull at your attention. You can complete the big thought later.

There are more things to notice.

Chapter Two

Meditation and Mental Illness

It happened to me sometimes when I went to Center City, Philadelphia at night, fixated on the red beacon flashing atop every skyscraper, and definitely when I visited Manhattan. For a while the lights and the sounds and the pace just took me, and before I knew it my mood was ablaze, my decisions poor, my sleep a short annoyance and my future barely considered. With each pulsing minute my impulse control deteriorated and my ability to make good choices took a thumping. The vibrant city would have been a great laboratory to study what it is that takes me as I turn manic, but I couldn't handle it and I was lucky when someone with me would whisk me away.

As I developed skill at noticing the physical feelings that seeped into my body as I ramped up, and as I became able to remain settled in a maelstrom of activity, my moods leveled and stayed still. Today the hum of the city still tunes me a pitch higher, but I can join the activity and not get carried away, literally and figuratively.

It was meditation that helped me develop the ability to approach a difficult or tempting situation and face it with the confidence that I could enter the fray and leave without scars on myself, my friends and family, or my wallet.

It's difficult to say how meditation has changed me, but it has changed my ability to cope with and manage the most challenging aspects of bipolar disorder. Mental illnesses are diseases of symptoms with indeterminate causes. The physical mechanisms that make one person ill while most others remain well are unclear. We speculate that there are genetic predispositions in there, and the brain of a person with an affective disorder must somehow be different than the brain of a person without one, but physical tests that prove the origin and development of many mental illnesses are elusive. Signs are absent. Symptoms are all we have.

And so we treat the symptoms and hope the disease goes away.

Meditation gives us a way to manage symptoms when they appear. It also enables us to catch presenting symptoms early and head off an impending episode of anxiety, depression or mania. But really, how?

We're in training when we practice meditation, developing the skill to bring focus and balance back to a situation with one deeply felt calming breath. This pause of flight, this ability to pull a field of scattered, slipping awareness back to one moment of hyper-attention and peace, enables us to pause and assess situations with a clear mind and an educated decision-making capacity. This all can happen in one breath. But only if we take thousands of focused breaths in practice first.

It may seem outrageous that one can pause the onslaught of emotion as mood changes take hold, but the ability to do just that is uncanny and can be developed. As this skill is developed through disciplined daily practice, it becomes clear how meditation can help battle mental illness on two fronts. The first is to help a person to settle down, pause and recover during a tumultuous period of budding anxiety, depression or mania. Caught early and contemplated, these forays into madness can be diminished and calmed before they take deep hold and drive a person into helpless distress. Episodes can be managed and made less damaging.

The second skill, harder to develop, precedes the first. One can actually predict when episodes are brewing. One can feel precursors in the body and in thoughts and emotions that foretell a slip in the mind's true functioning. There are always warning signs that an episode is imminent. While it may feel like dangerous mood changes just happen all of a sudden, more often telltale events occur first. But in the bustle of each day we miss them and end up sick. When we meditate and hold our attention on our body and mind, we can notice these markers that tip us off to trouble ahead. Then we can focus on the benefits of meditation and add other interventions as necessary to head off an episode or diminish its severity.

It's the Thoughts About Things, Not the Things Themselves

I've mentioned noticing things a few times, and this is the key to using meditation to help manage a mental illness. It's also the most powerful skill learned during any practice in focused attention.

In meditation you'll notice that often it's thoughts about things, not the things themselves, that stress you out. A bad situation at work, for instance, may need to be corrected. But while you're working on change, chewing on the anger and resentment caused by the situation will negatively impact your health far more than any event that caused you stress in the first place (abuse is different, and requires more than just meditation to help heal). With meditation you can notice how self-defeating these thoughts are and how they impact you, and work to expose them as just thoughts not always reflective of your reality. Especially with anger and judgment, we hold on to damaging ideas long after what caused the ideas to germinate has occurred, and we suffer terribly for it.

If thoughts are the causes of the worst of stress, it's good to practice with them, watch them pop up, notice if you create or exaggerate problems, and let all that go. Most episodes of affective disorders begin with a stress response. If these stressors are internally generated, it can only help to expose them as such and get on with what we can change, and deal more skillfully with the things we can't. The ability to still the mind and balance between conjecture and reality comes with serious meditation practice.

When you meditate, realize which of your thoughts are accurate reflections of your experience and which are hokum. Understand how you position events occurring in your life, or events that occurred in your past, and how this positioning influences your behavior and moods. As moods change, measure your thoughts and place what you're thinking into proper context. As you label thoughts that come up, pause and consider whether each thought rings true or rings hollow. Begin to know yourself. Be aware of how thoughts and, with them, your self-definition changes with your moods or level of anxiety.

That's fundamental, and you can run with that for a long time. Once you've exposed the fact that your identity and experience are made up of thoughts and that many, if not most, of those thoughts are in error, you can add a completely new perspective to your self-image. Just by sitting and focusing on the breath, you can reveal that much of who you think you are is a bunch of thoughts strung together, one contradicting the other.

Episodes of anxiety, depression or mania rarely appear without some predictive impulse. The slide into an episode can be gradual with lots of warning signs or precursors. Unfortunately, we usually miss all of them. While thoughts may be the most obvious and tangible signals of episodes, these warning signs are rarely just thoughts. Precursors to episodes often include physical symptoms which, when they appear, signal changes in mental health. Difficult emotions arise, too. The body, our emotions and our thoughts line up to form the perfect storm, and before we know it, an episode that challenges us rages out of control.

I remember my first psychotic break. I was a businessperson flying all over the country trying to turn around a challenged brand. The stress was unbearable, but I bore it, and rode right into psychotic mania. However, a lot of things went wrong before my reality ripped apart. Little things added up to one big break. I should have noticed. I could have acted on any one of them if I knew then what I know now. But it was my first time and it was all new.

Physical symptoms came first. I had problems with my gut that were diagnosed as irritable bowel syndrome and diverticulitis. I flexed between cramping discomfort and pain, and cooking and eating, which I had enjoyed so much, became a burden. Then came pains in my upper back and shoulders that were first attributed to all the luggage I hauled around. I consulted a neurologist who diagnosed fibromyalgia. He prescribed Naproxyn.

I became numb to all pleasure and started to spend money indiscriminately. My outlook dimmed and I started to think very dark thoughts as things that had brought me joy began to only agitate me. I wanted to tear apart the company for which I worked that had been so good to me. The neurologist then prescribed Prozac. I began to drink a lot and hallucinations crept into my field of vision. I lost all impulse control and became a cheat. I saw myself only as a destroyer, all dark and manic. I planned suicide and applied for a gun permit, but ended up committed to a psychiatric hospital before I could act.

Today the progression seems predictable, and I learned from my early experience. Repeated episodes followed the same pattern. Similar sensations and thoughts still arise. Only now when they do I'm able to notice them because I pay attention when I meditate. Meditating has led me to pay attention even when I'm not meditating, even when I'm active. Today each precursor seems so obvious. I'm able to notice them early. I can then put into place a plan my doctor and I worked out in advance to head off a serious mixed-episode. This has worked for me for years.

The key is to notice the warning signs and then counter them with calculated interventions. It really does work, but it takes some trial and error to discover how.

It wasn't obvious to me at first what my warning signs were. Memories of episodes were sketchy. I had some recall of the first break, and a few after that, but I had to carefully review my experience and identify the stages I went through as my mind crumbled. For me, it always starts with physical symptoms. Beside the gut problems and the pains, I'll sometimes get a strange sensation as if I've had way too much coffee, and my sleep patterns will be disrupted. In fact, the nervous feelings and changes in the amount or quality of my sleep are often the most telling.

These all seem obvious, but as the physical symptoms appear my mind is twisting into the seductive allure of spiraling mania or the deafening silence of depression. Or, as is often the case, both at the same time. It's easy to miss even the most severe signals in these moods.

My wife and daughter often accuse me of being grumpy, but as my moods shift I become downright curmudgeon-like. I lose all sense of happiness, and a reactive negative mood sets in that can suck all the joy out of the room. The ill feeling in my body intensifies. I always feel unsettled and fidgety.

Often my reading interests change. I read a lot, at least a book a week. I'll be engrossed in Shakespeare cover versions and suddenly shift into an obsession with economic history or biography. This may just as completely be replaced by a need to devour gothic fiction. These changes may be so sudden and complete that I may feel them mid-book and move on to something different.

Like a new book, I may take up a new hobby and go all in with the equipment and the time. Then I'll just as quickly drop it and latch on to something else. It's not a healthy interest in things. It's a place to pour money and attention and I end up ignoring everything and everybody else when I'm so distracted by a new, transient interest.

A strange psychosis sets in, and my body seems to separate from my mind and I become hyper-religious. Everything seems otherworldly, and I dive deeply into overidentification with some faith, or the occult, which on good days barely interests me.

Finally, in contrast to being grumpy inside the house, I'll confuse and upset my family by becoming boisterous and charismatic to people I barely know. I can be the life of the party, full of wit and energy, while my family suffers alone.

One or more of these things takes me early as I ramp up or slide down into intense mood changes. In the past I'd become dangerous and a hospitalization would follow. Today I've identified these precursors through practice, and having identified them, I'm able to notice them quickly as I meditate for a half-hour each day. Noticing such things and then acting on them makes serious episodes rare, and rarely disruptive. Today this system works so well that episodes are all but gone, and never dangerous. Constant practice has even made the symptoms and mood changes become milder.

A Clear Picture

When I meditate, a careful survey of the feelings in my body will expose any discomfort or unusual aches. My mood can be established, and thoughts that repeat often, and their labels, are noticed and noted. In this way I know that things are changing, and intervention may be necessary.

A plan goes into effect. I'll take something my doctor prescribed to help me regulate my sleep. I'll surrender my credit cards to my wife, who I've made aware of the budding episode, and rely on her for reports of how my behavior may be changing. She's often already clued in by my behavior. I'm often reluctant to accept her observations at first. It's tempting to deny another foray into madness. But careful introspection during contemplation and meditation usually reveals that she is correct.

I'll tighten up my routine, skip the wine with dinner, and add another meditation session each day to help stay calm and steady, and to notice how the changes, good and/or bad, are coming along. Often, this is enough to turn my mood back to its steady, normal state. If it's not, I'll contact my doctor. He can recommend more drastic but needed measures to rein me in.

It has gone on like this for about a dozen years. When I first implemented this system and began to succeed I was unmarried, so even though I rely heavily on my wife today, it can work without the observations of someone so close. I have taught this method to others and it has worked for them, too. You just need some careful introspection to identify your precursors and your triggers.

Leveling things out makes for a much more fulfilling life and can set you up for consistent success on all fronts. I'm suspicious of people who don't try because they "miss the highs" or think they'll lose their creative impulses and skills without the turbulent moods. I'd much rather always have the capacity to work with discipline and have the awareness to judge what is truly creative and what is beneficial to others, as opposed to efforts that are a waste of time. Good ideas will keep coming if you're consistent and you consistently apply your talents. There is no romance in insanity.

Focused attention and the realization that thoughts are illustrative but not always accurate can help reveal the harsh judgment we direct at ourselves when we fail, and help us overcome the doubts and insecurities we hatch when we succeed. A clear picture of one's present reality is attainable, and if that reality is troubling, one can successfully change it.

The Path of Meditation

There are steps along the path to bring the full force of

meditation to bear on a mental illness. To navigate these steps is to help predict episodes by noticing changes in physical and emotional health. Given some time spent practicing, one can avoid episodes entirely.

The first step is simply what most people seek from meditation: a calm mind. Time spent sitting quiet and still, focusing on the breath or a mantra or an object, may lead to some agitation and discomfort at first. But as skill at focusing attention and releasing the mind's hold on tenacious thoughts is developed, the mind will calm down and the body will relax into most periods of practice. As one becomes more adept at meditating, the ability to calm the mind by placing one's attention on the breath or another point of focus at all times, not just while sitting, will develop. The entire undertaking, after all, is practice for that. By using the word "practice," we acknowledge that we are out to learn something or to develop some skill. What we learn is the ability to balance thoughts and emotions and security within the body, achieved through diligent effort at calming the mind.

It may seem odd that it takes such effort to calm something down, but an unfocused mind will jump around like an excited puppy, and will be just as difficult to calm down. Also, especially in those of us with a mental illness, a mind focused on something unhealthy, something defeating or dangerous, will be hard to fracture and free. It's difficult to return to a state of calm that is necessary to achieve the balance required to live successfully with a mental illness. With consistent practice this skill can be developed.

Having a calm mind does not mean having a mind that sits in port for want of wind. A balanced mind can sail free and far and remain extremely creative as it works toward the challenges of big ideas. Calm in this sense does not mean dulled or tired, it means focused, mind opened up and settled down, ready for work.

The work performed during meditation, the next step along the path of practice, is insight. Here's where the calm mind takes flight in a good way. A person is able to fathom where they are, what influences them, and where they may be in error or treading too close to trouble. Insight is inhibited by limited vision and false ideas. A calm mind is prepared for more developed and encompassing vision and, as thoughts are examined for their veracity, false ideas are exposed for what they are. A path toward truth emerges.

Insight lies along this path. It may be an insight into how lies the mind is telling you fuel anxiety or depression, or it may be insight that reveals an episode of anxiety, depression or mania is on the launchpad and counting down to blast-off unless some well-thought-out changes are made quickly.

Insight will shine very bright light on ways we taunt and commit to behavioral changes, even when we try to remain level. Take, for example, anxiety. An individual can become so anxious that they will sit uneasy, convinced that they are going to die. But insight revealed through practice enlightens them to the fact that they don't die. In fact, one soon realizes that this panic is what fuels this distress more than any external event. The thoughts of coming apart add kindling to the fire of anxiety. Careful introspection of the false reveal of one's thoughts can help put this fire out. In an odd way, fully experiencing the internal thoughts and feelings of anxiety during meditation and discovering that often thoughts are behind the terror and the surrender can help one overcome anxiety and live more peacefully and secure.

Insight is a benefit of a mature meditation practice. It's both beautiful and exciting to make discoveries about your mental health in this way. We can always learn about our world and our place in it, and always adjust our opinions of the world and ourselves to best fit facts instead of some internally generated fiction.

The path that travels through insight approaches experience, the best teacher from whom a person can learn.

"Experience" can be a tricky word. To some it implies something we have, something developed over time. This view of experience looks toward the past at insight gathered as we have learned. Such insight and experience are valuable, and collected well can make us each truly informed. But to manage a mental illness, to predict an episode as it approaches, we need something more present and less reliant on the past. Yes, a survey of things that happened in the past will signal what we must look out for today, but our insight, experience and actions must be more present.

The realm of experience of interest here are events that take place right now: particular instances of personally encountering or undergoing something. To experience is an action. I experience things as they happen. I notice them and sense them. I comprehend them. I take them back into my mind and body where they are most deeply felt and truly measure my thoughts, feelings and emotions as they add up to the present state of the world and my place in it. We are our experience of the world. This world can be very small and not extend beyond our influence, or it can be huge and encompass all the people and things we care for and act on, plus everything else that distracts or enlightens us. It simply must be comprehended as it happens for experience to be realized.

A calm mind leads to insight, and this insight is tied to, and defined by, our present experience. To be present is to notice what is going on without this realization being polluted by fears and assumptions, expectations and limitations, of our past actions or inactions. It is also not interrupted by a projection of the present, or worse, the past, into the future. Yes, we learn from our mistakes and successes and we plan for further success, but to be truly present to our experience, to experience what is actually happening to us and in our world, is to enable ourselves to act in such a way as to properly handle the immediate challenges we seek to mitigate so that the worst of our mental illness will not again be expressed.

We experience the feelings in our bodies, the emotions that embody us, and the thoughts that trouble or stimulate our mind. In this experience we can predict a coming episode or turn down the intensity of a raging episode. Meditation makes us aware of what's happening and gives us the space to skillfully respond to our reality. Knee-jerk reactions will only make things worse. With a calm mind, insight and awareness of our experience, we can halt the reactions that send us headlong into trouble. We can then implement a plan that will keep us healthy and stable.

Meditation is a way to escape the tight grip of mental illness and to heal. When healed, and only then, can we grow and open up to the potential that life holds for us. It's a journey to wellness, and growth will begin along the way. The goal is a stable, creative, compassionate and vital life that we can share with others. If you can get better, it is your duty to get better. If you don't right away, please keep trying. The mark we leave can be a desirable one.

Chapter Three

How to Meditate

To Begin

Daniel Goldman writes that "meditation is an antidote to the mind's vulnerability to toxic emotions." It holds many benefits for those struggling to manage a mental illness. The obvious are stress management and improved focus. Others, such as regulation of emotions and revelation of the ability to predict difficult episodes, are also available to the meditator.

Meditation is quite different from sitting there doing nothing, thinking nothing. It is instead a focused attention on one's present experience. It offers a chance to observe your thoughts and the feelings in your body, and to contemplate that thoughts that are so influential to your emotions and your behavior may also be erroneous.

Meditation gives you the space to know and to change. It trains you to notice things you may have missed, and to find a still point in the onslaught of emotions a painful or scattered episode of anxiety, depression, or mania may bring. Simple in practice, it still requires effort to achieve real benefits.

So how does one begin?

There are many methods. Some focus on mantras or objects. But I find those methods often disregard feelings in the body and keep the focus in the head. I use a method similar to something called *zazen* that employs my own breath as the point of focus. This makes the body preeminent and downplays the duality of body and mind. It's worked for people for centuries, and has been promoted extensively by great minds as varied as Dogen in medieval Japan and Elaine MacInnes in a convent in Toronto in the twenty-first century.

Some sit cross-legged on a cushion on the floor. This does

provide a stable, supportive base and opens up the body for natural, unforced breath, but it is not necessary if it doesn't work for you. Sitting on a chair, if more comfortable, can also provide a stable base for practice. Just sit forward on the seat, rest your feet firmly on the floor, and position your spine erect, shoulders back, chin tucked, head gently pressed up toward the ceiling. If you can without painful discomfort, hold this position without support from the back of the chair.

If even that isn't possible because of physical challenges, lean back or even lie down. The point is to be dignified and still, and to breathe naturally. Remember, proper posture is important to align the body and, with it, the mind. What to do with your hands can be a special distraction, so just fold them gently in your lap or place the palms down on your thighs.

In this position, focus on the breath. Breathe naturally through the nose, in and out, unless it's clogged. Focus on the breath wherever in the body you feel it the most. Always scan the body while you breathe. Counting breaths can help keep the focus on the breath, so count each breath, up to ten. Then begin again at one.

Other tips include closing your eyes to increase your focus on the breath, or gazing in soft focus at a spot on the floor a few feet in front of you. Or you may want to stare at a blank wall. Holding the eyes in soft focus will reduce blinking, but you'll find that even if your eyes are closed, you still blink. Meditation is full of surprises from your body that you never noticed before. Gently close your mouth, teeth slightly apart, and position your tongue behind your top teeth to reduce swallowing.

Just remember, we're not taking a nap. We're falling awake.

Focus on the breath, feeling the rise and fall of the belly, the subtle expansion and contraction of the chest and back, keeping the breath natural, not forcing it or trying to slow it down or breathing deeply. This is a practice to experience the present moment as it is, and although it may relax you, it is not a relaxation exercise. Keep everything as it naturally occurs and always return the attention to the breath.

Thoughts will tumble through your mind and constantly pull your attention away from the breath. The mind will wander all over the place, and even after years of practice, thoughts will continue to interrupt. Just notice that you are thinking, let the thought go, and return the attention again to the breath. If you're counting breaths and you've lost your count at three or four, or you find yourself at fifteen or twenty-seven when you meant to stop at ten, just let it go and begin again at one.

You'll find yourself constantly distracted by your thoughts. You'll notice you've drifted off and have to return to the breath, over and over. In a way, since you keep losing your place and thoughts keep pulling you away from your count and your breath, meditation becomes an exercise in failure. As Samuel Beckett wrote: "Ever tried. Ever failed. No matter. Try again. Fail again. Fail better."

Stick with it. Even when you think you're terrible at it.

Discomfort is another challenge. If you find an itch, don't scratch it. Just focus your attention into that spot and experience the itch. If you feel bearable pain in your shoulder, or legs, or anywhere, do not reposition. Just direct your attention to that part of your body that aches and focus on release with each exhale. Hold your position, focus on the breath, and experience the body in full. If you find a position becomes too painful, then respect the body and make adjustments as necessary.

Be kind to yourself and don't be overly ambitious. In the beginning, you may only be able to hold this attention for a few moments. The thoughts may become too much, or the body too uncomfortable. Although today I meditate for 30 minutes each day, I began at only 5 minutes, and it took a long time to work up from there. Just be aware that any period of focused attention is valuable, and persevere.

That's it. You don't need apps or books or expensive courses, although a good teacher can help if you hit a difficult patch of thoughts or feelings. Do it every day and the benefits will accrue to you. Meditating like this is as simple as breathing, and as natural. And while it has been a challenge at times, over the years nothing has helped me manage my bipolar disorder better.

Breathing

When you follow your breath you anchor your mind, emphasize feelings in your body and gain great insight into your emotions. By varying the breath you can actually change your mood or calm anxiety, or refocus attention and bring a wandering mind back to the present, back to a point of focus. Breathing is the one function of the autonomic nervous system that we can consciously vary. We can speed it up, slow it down, or make it full or shallow. The unconscious mind and physical movement can influence heartbeat, blood flow and digestion, but only breathing can you vary with a simple decision and very little effort. In meditation, the point is to notice the breath and use it to corral a wandering mind.

While you meditate, breathe naturally. Don't force the breath or consciously try to change it. It may feel good to take a couple of deep breaths and relax into a period of meditation, but it's important to just experience the breath as it is at this time. The breath can yield great insight into the state of your mind. You'll notice that different patterns of breathing match different moods, and noting these patterns can tip you off to a change in your physical or mental health.

The breath offers two excellent places to focus on to keep the attention fixed during the period that you meditate. Place your attention in your nostrils and notice that they cool as you inhale and warm again with each exhale. Stay with this feeling and feel the variance in temperature while breathing naturally. Another profound spot to place your attention is deep in the abdomen, where there's a pause between each inhale and each exhale. Feel fully the inhale and notice that just for a moment breathing stops before the exhale begins. You may find that by concentrating on either of these physical sensations of breathing your mind may wander less. Or, you'll have a definitive spot of feeling to return to when your attention slips away and your focus lags.

You may also notice that thoughts adjust slightly from inhales to exhales. The inhale may feel more panicked and the exhale more secure. Moods serve up many physical feelings, whether it's the agitation of anxiety, the surrender of depression or the racing of mania. These sensations are more deeply felt as you draw the breath in. A more normal feeling on the exhale illustrates to you how meditation can calm your mind and give you the opportunity to tame an episode as it takes you.

When surveying the body during meditation, the breath can be used to fully experience relaxation or discomfort. Legs will often ache. Shoulders tend to creep up as if wanting to fold into the meditator's ears. Odd places where one holds tension and stress will be revealed: maybe the jaw, or the gut, or the forehead. When tension is found it helps to direct the attention, through the breath, to the troubled spot in the body. Imagine breathing into that spot, and relaxing on the exhale.

Breathing may be most effective at helping us establish a point of reference, or an anchor, for the attention. In meditation we practice releasing distractions and bringing the attention back to the breath. Whether it's terror or pain or dullness that we encounter, we can let the troubling thoughts and sensations go and return to the breath. With this practice we can become adept at applying this skill to all situations in life, even when not meditating. The breath is always available for us to refer to and to focus on, freeing us of distraction and disturbances that ruin our experience of what we engage in in the present moment.

Counting Breaths

When I teach meditation, I often recommend counting breaths to keep the attention focused on the breath. Most teachers' methods are similar, all some variation of counting to ten. Some recommend counting inhales and exhales; others count only exhales. Most count each breath from one to ten and then start over again at one. Another method has the meditator count exhales to ten, and then count exhales down from nine to zero. Repeat. But you get the point. Focus on the breath by counting each breath. If you lose your count, or realize you've counted past ten because your mind has wandered, just return to one and start over.

But sometimes the counting becomes so automatic, so routine, that I can count from one to ten and repeat, barely noticing the count, my mind wandering all the while. Little work with focused attention is being done. To counter this, I learned a very effective counting method from neurosurgeon and Zen practitioner James Austin at a workshop on Zen and the Brain.

Dr Austin presents his counting method as the "Just This" method. To begin, on each inhale think *Just*, and on each exhale count a number, again one through ten. Do this as long as you wish or can, until you get bored or things become too automatic, or until you keep losing your place and get frustrated. Then change each inhale to *This* and continue to count each exhale. This method helps one focus on the breath and reinforces the whole point of sitting and meditating. Just one. Just a breath. This one. This breath. Then, when you wish, inhale on *Just* and exhale on *This*. Just this breath. When you wish or must, you can start again. You may even wish to breathe for a while with no count or words. Just focus on the breath as it comes, as you can. Mix it up as you wish, but keep the attention focused on the breath. When you find thoughts taking your attention away, let them go and return to the breath. Over and over again.

Practicing this way has made me more aware of my mind wandering. I don't think my mind is wandering more using this method, I just think I'm noticing it more accurately than I did before. This has helped make my focus my breath. After I notice I'm distracted and have to bring my attention back to the breath, I feel things with more intensity.

What to Do with All of These Thoughts?

It's easy to say that when meditating one should focus on the breath and release thoughts as they arise, but it's incredibly difficult to do. There are times when I'm hypomanic and ideas fly through my head. Concentration and attention are very difficult. Acknowledging thoughts and letting them go is hard enough on a good day. At times like that I wonder *What do I do now?*

During meditation you keep your attention on your breath, but you want to be fully aware in this moment. You still take note of sounds and smells, aches and pains, all that makes up your present awareness. When thoughts arise, the instructions are to notice them, let them go and return to the breath and your awareness of all that is around you. But to just blot out thoughts without paying attention to them would not be very mindful at all, and it would not help you predict your episodes.

As a thought pops up, acknowledge it as you let it go, and return to the breath. Don't carry it out to a conclusion. Don't dwell on it. Don't begin a conversation with yourself about it. Don't try to add reason at this time. Notice that you're thinking, that your mind has pulled you away from your awareness of this moment, and place your attention back on the breath.

Labeling thoughts may help you release them. If you sit stewing about something you should have done differently this morning, label it "judging" and let it go. If you think about what to make for lunch or what to do this weekend, label that "planning" and return to the breath. If you're taken by thoughts of beaches and the sun, label them "fantasy" and bring your attention back to the present moment. The point is never to not think. The point is to remain aware of what is going on in and around you right now. Too many scattered thoughts can drag you away from the moment and cheat you of your present experience. They'll also make it difficult to notice the physical signals of an oncoming episode. Acknowledge thoughts, label them, and come back to the present. This will help you stay centered and focused.

As for the encounters with hypomania of which I wrote, practice makes me aware that the flight of ideas that comes with hypomania has taken hold. Before I became a meditator, these thoughts would have tumbled out of control, and my attention, mood and behavior would have suffered. But being aware of what is happening in the world I'm in right now, and having some practice in how to let thoughts go, helps me to keep things under control. It also allows me to properly monitor the situation and to be prepared to act if the simmering hypomania becomes more serious. I'm still agitated, my mind still keeps me up at night, but I'm as aware that what is taking me now are just thoughts as I am aware that my breath is always available — available to draw my attention and return me to my present experience, even if it's an uncomfortable one. I'm also aware that if I stay focused, I'll know when to intervene with help from others, and from medicine, if this exuberant feeling gets a little too intense.

Part of what meditation can be is practice for a crisis. Practice at letting go of random and confusing thoughts. If you can learn to keep your attention on your breath and in the present on a good day, then you can use this technique to remain grounded when things get difficult. The mind can hold great escapes, but we must always return to the present. Staying in the present as often as possible can help us avoid the wreckage that can occur when our minds take us too far from what is really happening at this very moment.

The Mind Lies; the Body Tells the Truth

Meditation is not exclusively for what is in your head. In fact, an over-focus on one's experience with thoughts, ignoring the physical experience of deep focus, leads the meditator to miss most of what's going on at present. For while thoughts seem to be in the forefront to an unskilled meditator, most of what's going on is physical. Physical expression of the body and the body's place in the physical world are keys to awareness and experience. The most telling signs that an episode is upon you will be found in your body, not in your head.

For me, thoughts go sour quickly before an episode begins, and my thought patterns break, so I'm likely to buy into or act on the poor judgment my mind hoists on me. As an episode begins, I can't trust my mind, and I can't always notice the truth about my mind and its actions.

Long before my thoughts change, in a lead-up to the darkening or frantic acceleration of my moods, changes occur in my body. There's a picture of me at my sister's wedding sitting with her and my brothers. It was taken just days before I attempted suicide. In the picture I'm slumped; shoulders collapsed; spine curved; head flopped to one side like a worn-out rag doll. If I had been a meditator then, sitting with proper posture while practicing, I would have noticed the slouch that had overtaken me. I would have noticed that I had caved in. I could have done something about it. But I was not physically aware, and by the time the photos were developed and presented in an album for everyone to see, it was too late.

Physical changes almost always precede the mental ones. The body leads the mind. When the body is ignored, so are one's truest thoughts, emotions and impulses. To know yourself requires an intimate knowledge of your entire being. Seeing the body as something separate from the self is a sure path to poor mental health.

In your body, not in your thoughts, resides all you cherish, feel and risk. People with mental illness often die young. Sure, some succumb to suicide, the ultimate attack on one's body, but most die early from diseases that are comorbid with psychiatric disease: so-called physical chronic illnesses like diabetes, obesity or heart disease. Mental illness is as much a physical disease as any of these. The stress we feel that sets off our worst episodes is an event that riddles the entire body. It's no wonder that in both classical Chinese and biblical Hebrew there is one word that means both heart and mind: *xin* (Chinese) and *leb* (Hebrew). One can't be sick in one or the other; one is sick in both at once.

If you want to discover the truth in the physical changes that fuel anxiety, stop trying to intellectually figure out your emotions. Feel them, experience them fully. Don't deny them. You may not be able to put labels on what you encounter, you may find sensations beyond words. You'll know in your body. You'll feel better or you'll feel worse. But you'll feel. Our bodies hold many of the answers to what we feel and what we need. To feel experience is a physical sense. Our bodies already know our experience in a pre-linguistic manner. You're likely to feel distress before you think it. It's the animal in our selves expressed.

Our hunter-gatherer ancestors were always aware. Threats and famine forced them to be forever vigilant. Their fight-or-flight response was hardwired and helped them meet threats and seize opportunities to survive. The fight-or-flight response is a series of physiological changes that occur when we are threatened or highly stressed. A flood of hormones and neurotransmitters and redirected blood flow consume us as we enter a state of hyperarousal, ready for attack.

Even though our world is so far removed from the one our ancestors knew, the fight-or-flight response remains with us.

Threats and stressors in our modern civilization may be less immediately life-threatening, but grinding constant effort over how we organize society and ourselves and how we fit into our interconnected but sometimes uncaring world still triggers the physiological response all the same. People with mental illness may be especially tuned in to these simmering threats.

The fight-or-flight response enabled us to react quickly in the face of a grave threat. Threats have changed over millennia, but the physiological response remains the same. To our bodies, a bear at the door or the possibility of losing a marriage prompt the same physical response; the same rush of neurotransmitters and redirection of blood flow. For our ancestors, the bear at the door either killed them or went away. Or they killed it and feasted. Either way the stressor was removed and they returned to a healthy unstressed state of homeostasis. Today the stressors never seem to end. We worry incessantly about our children, our jobs, our relationships. We despise our commutes. We stay highly charged and hot-wired in full fight-or-flight mode always, and while the end with the bear came quickly, this modern stress will kill us or make us crazy over time, maybe a long time, and with pain both psychic and physical.

That's why meditation, or focused attention, can't be a temporary thing you do for a period of time each day. Those 20 to 30 minutes of practice each day must be applied. You should try to pay attention all the time. Focus can infuse your day. Try to be forever vigilant and aware and relaxed and balanced, or the stressors will pile on and you'll suffer dearly. All of the time. Even as you review events and plan responses, remain present and fully aware of what your body tells you.

To be inattentive and forgetful is to invite thoughts to drift astray, sometimes into dangerous places. The body will tense and tighten, unnoticed. Stress pushes us into our heads, into panicked thoughts, as our bodies get sick. When I'm stressed, I get so caught up in a terror of thoughts that it seems my body doesn't even exist. But everything is physical.

Most episodes of mania, depression or anxiety are stress responses. We are forced into reactivity. If you're tuned in to the body while meditating, you will notice the physical expression of this reactivity to stress before your mind gets wrapped up in it. Then, the calm mind aspect of meditation will help you stay balanced if the stress worsens, and the insight aspect of meditation will give you some bearing on what to do next. It will help you determine how to properly deal with the stress you've discovered; the stress that aims to trigger your mental illness.

God or nature or both gave us this body through which we experience the world. Even if our thoughts are in error and our self-definition is false, the body and its interactions with the environment remain very real. Through these interactions the mind can be healed. I know through my body when an episode of mania or depression is coming. I know through my body that my mind is brewing inconsistencies or I'm making poor decisions. The actions of my body are easier to notice than the thoughts that occur with them, so by living fully within my body, by paying attention to and feeling every fiber of my being, I can best know the state of my mental health.

Is the Mind Really Always Fibbing?

Our reason makes us uniquely human. It joins with our sense of spirit to help us fathom and achieve our potential. But in mental illness, our reason can be clouded or broken. Meditation deep within the body can reveal truth and help us measure when our reason holds up to inspection and when it fails.

Human minds have combined with free will to give us everything from material comfort to human rights. The mind also has a unique ability to recognize when it doesn't work, and to develop and follow therapies that fix it. But still, for most of us, much of what we think is either incorrect or incomplete. This both gets us into trouble and gives us incredible opportunities to improve. Noticing this is how we make good decisions and gain wisdom. But minds break. A disabled mind has the potential to magnify errors and miss obvious answers.

The world has been changed by really big, really good ideas, and sitting and contemplating things can result in one realizing tremendous truths. So why do I say that the mind lies and most thoughts are erroneous? Because most of them are. For every good idea I've ever had, I've had dozens of bad ones. That's OK for brainstorming or trying to be creative. Many ideas falter. As soon as we recognize that, we can begin to notice the good ones. Benjamin Rush said: "The human mind seldom arrives at truth upon any subject, till it has first reached the extremity of error." For every truth I've ever realized, I've waded through countless layers of BS in getting there. And most of that BS was generated by my own mind.

Unfortunately, much of the inaccuracy presented by my mind to my mind is about myself. Much of that is damaging to my self-image and my self-definition. We can be masters at self-deception, representing ourselves and our realities as a fiction we create and keep deep inside. Then we start to believe it. Meditation can help when our internal narrative strays far from the truth.

It doesn't take much to get a person worrying about how well they're doing. Whether it's on a job or on a date, self-judgment can be very critical and likely exaggerates faults that seem very small to, or are not even noticed by, others. The mind exaggerates threats so we're sure to notice them. That's nature. We're hyper-focused on our failings, and things that can go wrong, so we can skillfully self-correct. This can help a healthy mind get things right when the dust of defeating whispers settles. But those whispers can turn into screams in a troubled mind, and it's easy to disappear down a long tunnel of all that is wrong with you, plus some. Then the mind adds on all that's not wrong with you and makes you think that it is.

This can get dangerous in a person with an affective disorder. In mixed-episodes I tend toward hyper-religiosity. Maybe it's my interest in vampire stories or intellectual biographies, but I'm always on the precipice of a nightmare. I start to think God is out to get me. When mania strikes depression in my mind, I latch on to things I've done wrong and position myself as evil. Of course, I'm not evil. I'm a good husband and a good dad, I work hard and hold to a high level of morality. I don't even steal sugar packets or creamers from the diner. But in my diseased mind I can quickly formulate ways in which I'm doomed and should be punished. That used to lead me to some very dark places.

Now, as I notice thoughts when I meditate and give those thoughts a little thought, I readily see that what my mind reveals to me is a bunch of bunk and a sure sign that I need to seek some help and get better. But it's not always that extreme. Little negative thoughts pop up constantly in most of us, and they can lead us right into depression or anxiety. These inaccurate stories we tell ourselves must be exposed as lies, because I bet most of the negative thoughts you have about yourself, and sometimes others, are either patently untrue or blown all out of proportion.

If the instruction for meditation is to encounter thoughts and let them go, how do you even begin to notice whether a thought is accurate or not? You don't spend enough time with it. Here, when you're skilled at focusing your attention, isolating and labeling thoughts and feeling all of the comfort and discomfort in your body, you can begin to introduce a bit of inquiry into your practice.

Zen teachers seem to doubt everything. The entire practice is one big question mark stamped on all one can encounter. This is healthy. The Psalms throw so many outrageous claims at the reader that one is forced to break through to how one really perceives the world of which they are a part. Meditation gives you the opportunity to sit with thoughts, emotions and feelings that bubble up and to ask, "What is this?" Notice thoughts that repeat, mull them over and be honest with yourself. Are things really that bad, or does thinking make it so? Are you taking small flaws or transgressions and turning them into monsters of self-hate, self-doubt and self-defeat? Why? What is that doing to your mental health?

Terrible things may have happened to you, or you may have done terrible things, and that may trap you in a spiral of illness and episodes that compromise all functioning. I don't want for a minute to imply that things from your past are behind you and you should just get over them. I would never minimize in that way the pain inflicted on you, or the pain you caused someone else. Those things may take years of therapy to reconcile and much faith to forgive, if that's even possible. I would like you to investigate how past events influence your present experience. If negative thoughts are tied to a person you used to be, shouldn't you consider who you are today and whether or not those negative thoughts hold up to current investigation and self-reflection? Sometimes thoughts about an event cause more suffering than the event itself.

Just as thoughts can fool us into thinking things are worse than they really are, they can shield us from how bad things have gotten. Don't be a Pollyanna. Go back into the body as a check on the ramblings of the mind.

While when well we may overestimate how bad things are, as an episode approaches we may convince ourselves that things are actually OK. No one wants to be sick again, yet the mind plagued by mental illness may pull toward dysfunction. Instead of fighting, or even noticing this pull, we all too often plunge into the worst our illness can deal us. At times like this it feels like we want to be sick. But we can check that. If we're going to doubt the self-defeating thoughts we have, we're also going to have to shine some very bright light on thoughts that say everything is OK. Just to be sure. Don't get insecure about it. Just check your feelings so you can be confident that you can trust them. Expose thoughts. See them for what they are. Isolate the lies you tell yourself and set them down.

Don't get trapped in your head as you subject yourself and your thoughts to deep inquiry while meditating. Stay in the body. If you discover an item that you're lying to yourself about, note how that feels. What does it do to your breathing or how you hold your shoulders? How does physically calming down or repositioning the body change your thought patterns? You'll find again that the body leads the mind, and by practicing within the body you'll more easily find out which memories or beliefs hold truth and which thoughts should be trusted or not. You'll feel it. Have some confidence in what your body tells you.

Muscle memory is a tremendous force. When you find inaccuracies in your thoughts by practicing healthy doubt and then go deep into the body, surprising things about yourself and your experience may surface. They may not always be pleasant, so be prepared. But all on its own the body will reveal truths too big for the mind to comprehend, and reveal lies too tucked away for the mind to notice.

In this way, working with the body and the mind as one, a fully unified force, you can discover what is true about your condition and your present life's circumstance. Naturally, and with some honest reflection to both yourself and others in whom you trust, you'll begin to see a way out of the trap of mental illness. You'll notice when your thoughts are dragging you into an episode, and through such an accurate survey of your thoughts and the feelings present in your body, you'll know when an episode is coming. Then you'll be able to act and stave off the worst of it. It's not easy. It takes a tremendous amount of practice. But it is possible and can make life so much more stable and productive. It can help you like yourself, and love others, too.

Contemplation

While many meditation traditions will stop at the exposure of reality for what it is, and the revelation that thoughts make up this reality and, possibly, our entire notion of self, I advocate taking the discoveries in your body and mind that you've uncovered while meditating and spending a little time reviewing them, and comparing them to how you feel or think on an average day.

Contemplate, or sit quietly and specifically think about, what you encounter. Reflect on what you discover and how it influences, or can explain, your mental health.

Perhaps this is too utilitarian for seekers of enlightenment or religious experience, but I want to get some immediate feedback on my state of being, especially when I notice things that may signal an oncoming episode of anxiety, depression or mania. I want to spend some time while I meditate, or ideally a few minutes after I meditate, in deep contemplation of what I encountered while I was still. Discovery is possible, and I may find I need to act in order to remain stable. This action may be a simple thought about my mood, or a fire alarm about a threat my mind places in my way. But this action will only be prompted by some time spent in an activity of focused attention. An activity such as meditation.

Some people keep dream journals and look to them to discover truths about their experience. A meditation journal can yield insight as well. Keep a pen and paper handy and, when you finish meditating, jot down what you feel in your body and what thoughts dog you. Concurrent with these notes, track your daily moods. Rate your mood from good to bad, from exuberant to depressed. Star days that are troublesome. Then overlap your mood-tracking notes with a record of how your body feels and the thoughts that persist in your meditation notes and see what jumps out at you. Do certain feelings or thoughts repeat on difficult days? Do you discover things to be aware of that may coincide with different moods? You likely will, and contemplating these things, these feelings and thoughts that reflect specific moods, will enable you to better balance your mental health by modifying your behavior to level your moods.

If you meet a good mood, make it a productive day. Or an introspective day. If you find your mood difficult, note the feelings in your body and the thoughts that bubble up and, when they repeat, act with an intervention that will help keep you safe.

Contemplation is how you leverage your experience into insight to discover how you truly feel and decide if there's anything you should do about it. Contemplation on your meditation sessions will reveal your progress toward stability.

Right now, you may be thinking that all of this meditation and contemplation aimed at managing moods will just make life dull and robotic. A person can be too level and not enjoy the waves of normal emotions, can't they? The point of the method I advocate is not to dull emotion but to enhance it. You can introduce enough stability that you can truly feel and personify the range of emotions encountered in a deep, vital life. Stability gives one the freedom to explore moods and their influences while not losing one's reason or ability to function and respond to the life illuminated by a healthy, wide range of emotions. Stability also enables us to be at our most creative. Our best work is done not when moods run untamed or when moods are extinguished, but when moods are well-managed.

Practice, reach out to others with what you learn, and stay healthy.

Chapter Four

Issues in Meditation

Silence?

People always look at me funny, especially when I teach in the city in my home in Philadelphia, when I tell them to sit in silence. The room where I meditate sits just a couple hundred feet from Interstate 95. The hum of traffic merges with the distant sirens and the wind in the trees and bird calls out my window to form a cacophonous white noise that washes over the house. If I pay particular attention, the noise separates into distinct, noticeable sounds, and I can focus on each of them. Here, as it seems everywhere, albeit with different interruptions, there is no silence.

There is no silence in silent places, either. I've been to monasteries in the mountains where the birds cawed louder than the most assertive noises of the city, and the cicadas at night roared in waves of audible aural assault. Silent work practice at one monastery was interrupted by strains of Metallica from a house down the hill. Another time, in a quiet office buried in the back of the rectory, church bells jolted me from dozing during a service of centering prayer.

Composer John Cage wrote music that included long periods of silence. When the musicians stopped playing, concertgoers were quickly confronted with the shuffling, shifting, and coughing sounds in the concert hall. There always seemed to be a solo performed by someone unwrapping a candy.

So what do all these meditation people mean when they say, "Sit in silence"?

One must allow for ambient noise. True silence is the absence of any introduced sound or sound painted onto the environment by the person seeking silence. Talking is an obvious interruption, but reading and writing also add layers of dissonance onto the silence we seek. Of course, anything one can turn on or off is introduced noise: phones, TVs, radios, computers, tablets. Whether the sound is on or muted, if they are on at all they disturb silence because they distract us from introspection. Even eye contact and hand gestures destroy silence. All of these things are banned from silent retreats. Anything we personally introduce to the world is noise and disrupts silence. All of this must be eliminated when meditation begins.

That's why I think meditation apps are not the best way to practice. How can you sit and notice your most internal voice, or quietly identify troubling signs of an oncoming problem, when you're anticipating the next thing the calming voice will say through your earbuds? Guided meditation has a place but often can be a distraction that keeps you from the truth and clarity you seek. Meditators have sat silently for centuries. Our modern technology can improve many things, but not everything. Certainly not the time-tested disciplines of meditation and contemplation. Just be quiet. All you seek will come to you. Or nothing will come. At least you'll notice.

The absence of introduced sound can make almost any activity an exercise in focused attention. This is a real boon to those who have difficulty with silent meditation. You can focus quietly anytime, anywhere. Our dishwasher broke nearly three years ago and, as odd as it sounds, I've come to treasure washing the dishes with all the media off and only the sound of the dishes clattering, the water and the sponge, and whatever is happening outside. We have yet to buy a new one.

Try to run or exercise without earbuds, only a focus on the increasing rhythm of the breath. Play with a pet or make love without introduced noise. Stop checking social media all the time. A new realm of communication opens up. One where distractions do not rule, and thoughts can be gently encountered and contemplated. Anything can be meditation.

Of course, meditation requires this quiet. Even those who use mantras most often repeat the sounds quietly in their heads. Chants and prayers are valuable spiritual practices, but for managing a mental illness, be sure silence is a part of your practice. Don't tempt yourself with distractions. For the chosen period of time spent sitting, the phone must be put away and silence enforced. I think you can do it for 20 or 30 minutes.

Or maybe not.

A study of 580 undergraduate students undertaken over six years shows that the constant accessibility and exposure to background media has created a mass of people who fear silence. This research by Drs Michael Bittman of the University of New England and Mark Sipthorp of the Australian Institute of Family Studies argues that "their need for noise and their struggle with silence is a learnt behavior."[1] This cannot be blamed on the relatively recent rise of social media and 24-hour connectivity. For so many of these students' lives the TV was always on, even when no one was watching, and that was often the case for their parents while growing up as well. If the background noise of media has always been with us, it's no wonder we can become so uncomfortable when it's taken away.

Lest I try to pass myself off as a contemplative or a meditation master, I confess that I have my own difficulty with silence. My wife and I, city dwellers, were once on vacation staying in a house far from the city. It was rustic, with no TV, radio or internet. When we went to bed it was so dark and quiet it was unsettling. We couldn't sleep! If I miss a few days meditating in a row, as I did when my routine was interrupted and the house was full early in the Covid-19 shutdown, I find it very challenging to break away and begin my practice again. And when I am in a difficult episode, riddled with self-doubt, nervousness or anxiety, the last thing I want to do is turn off all of the media or put down the books that distract me from my insecurity. But I soon realize that distractions can exacerbate the difficulty I face. I get back to fixed periods of silence, return to the discipline of my practice, and heal.

If the fear of silence is a learned behavior, it can be unlearned. This can be undertaken through meditation and focused attention. To develop focused attention, you may want to begin by confronting the experience of silence. Turn everything off, go to as quiet a place as you can find, and sit for a few minutes. Take in the environment. Just experience the present moment and allow what is around you to exert itself uncommented upon. If you find yourself agitated or ill-at-ease, notice that. Start with very short periods of quiet. Slowly, as silence is embraced, you will find comfort there.

Some people are convinced they can't do it. If silence is that uncomfortable for you, build up your meditation practice slowly. Sit silently for just a few minutes. Add a minute a day, or a week. Take as long as you need to work up to 20 to 30 minutes. Then stick with it. Trust me. You will come to treasure this respite of peace and quiet, and you will tap wells of creativity there that you didn't even know you had. Deep work, like the work of improving yourself and your mind and your relationships with others, is only possible in significant periods of silence.

Community

While meditation is a solitary practice, you shouldn't feel alone while doing it. For all the talk of self-care and I, me, mine that infuses the conversation about mindfulness (and infuriates people who don't see selfishness as a virtue), you're really practicing to be a better person for others; for those you love, for those in need and for society. If you can't think of anyone you love, or anyone who loves you, and if you feel completely cut off from society, do it for the community of other people just like you, for there are others with similar challenges—people who are trying, failing, and trying again. Just like you.

In community we are least likely to give up. That's the entire point of surviving and thriving with a mental illness. Community can be large, like a family, a church congregation or a support group, or it can be small, like a single friend or a therapist. Make relating to these people, listening to them and learning from them, part of your practice. Just be careful that the community you choose comes together for something positive, and not just against stuff, as so many groups force their way onto us today.

Meditation all too often conjures images of some solitary individual, unkempt and living in a cave on a mountain, deep in contemplation at all hours. These people did exist, from the desert fathers to Chinese hermits, and in some places probably still do, but most meditators throughout history meditated in large groups and in community.

In the Christian Church the very word "communion" establishes the eucharist as a communal meal, meant to bring people of God together. In Judaism a *minyan* of ten believers is required for a period of prayer. In Islam, five times a day, all believers stop what they're doing and pray toward Mecca, probably the biggest communal activity the world has ever known.

Buddhism established the three jewels, Buddha, Dharma, and Sangha. The placement of the Buddha is obvious, and the Dharma is the teaching. The Sangha is the community of practitioners, joined together to follow the eightfold path and support one another in practice. I fear too many Western lay practitioners of Buddhism have little contact with this jewel. You won't get to the beauty of service to others that wellness demands by embarking on a selfish, exclusively inward-focused journey.

It is a crime of the modern mindfulness industry that meditation seems an exercise in self-absorption focused on self-improvement and self-care, stroking with comfort one's own suffering, while ignoring the ethics that our practices exist to help others suffer less just as much, even more so, than we seek to help ourselves. I know all about the need to put your own oxygen mask on first in an emergency on a plane before helping someone sitting next to you, but the metaphor doesn't hold up in a spiritual sense. Every faith treasures self-sacrifice, from the concept of tithing to the Bodhisattva vow.

I was on a retreat when we entered a 36-hour period of silence. The night before, I told one of the leaders about my bipolar disorder and that the experience might be difficult for me, and that I might need some support. He nodded and smiled. Imagine my surprise the next morning when the leaders instructed the group to stay within their own experience and, should they witness someone break down, just survey their own reaction to the other's suffering. "Stay with yourself, feel your experience, don't reach out. This is about your inner self. Explore the sensations in your body and mind always." Well, I did break down and lay sobbing for hours in the back of the room, ignored. I had never felt so alone. At one point a woman walked over to me and laid her hand on my shoulder. It was as if an angel of God descended and assured me I had the strength to continue. There was more love in that touch than in the 450 people meditating completely within themselves, noticing nothing but their own breathing. It just seemed a sad lesson. Yes, I teach people to go deep within, but never to lose their connection to the community that supports them, and that relies on them for support.

One way to help you love yourself is to love everyone else. Everyone. Those close to you are easy. But love those you disagree with, too. Believe in the innate goodness of human nature. You need it to go on. You can learn from everyone, and if you reach out to people you'll be amazed at what comes back. Some people will disappoint or disregard you, especially if you're burdened with a serious mental illness. But there will always be someone willing to reach out to you and give back. Don't let them down. They'll stand by you. If they hurt you, realize you did all you could for them in love. Love that is for you as much as it is for the one you share it with.

Find community. Seek out groups to meditate with: at a centering prayer group or a Zen center, maybe a drop-in at a community center or a yoga studio. If no group exists, start your own. Include your family and those closest to you.

You have to draw on your own energy to overcome and manage a mental illness, and people will hurt you. Try not to hurt them, and find some people to be still with. You'll continue to work at your practice most often on your own. You'll still be looking inward. But don't be selfish with your meditation. Open up to others.

Connectivity

The marvels of technology available to nearly everyone in the world today are awe-inspiring. I'm not going to be a luddite and rail against what this technology hath wrought. Sitting in the doctor's waiting room I have access at my fingertips to the world's most up-to-date information available about my condition. I also have access to a lot of poorly researched opinion masquerading as fact. Ironically, it's hard to tell the difference without an expert like a doctor. Yet, information is so available and seemingly so complete that we have come to distrust experts who rely on the scientific method and often give us answers we don't always want to hear. Unless we question everything and check all sources, we can never be sure we're getting the truth. But who has time for that? That's why you need to find a good doctor you can work with, develop a treatment plan together, and stick with it, despite what someone without credentials writing a blog will tell you.

Interconnectivity also makes us feel more important than we are. Don't misunderstand me. I think individual liberty reigns supreme and that every person has innate value. No one is more important than your closest circle of family and friends, and technology to keep you in touch can help build bonds. But paradoxically, the same technology meant to bring us together can drive us apart and kill our empathy. So many people are online posting information about themselves and the tiniest details of their lives. They are sharing information that reinforces opinions they have already told their network countless times. They make their lives look so complete and full. And they almost never reach out to individuals and sincerely ask, "How are you?"

It seems we all have something to say and no one is asking one another the most simple questions about their inner life. It seems people only care about themselves and how others perceive them on the media they share. No wonder rates of mental illness are skyrocketing.

It's not all bad. There are tremendous opportunities to develop and join communities online. Supportive meditation groups, especially those practicing Western methods of meditation, can be difficult to find. An organization like World Community for Christian Meditation reaches people worldwide with resources that can support far-flung practitioners. Lectures from all traditions' greatest teachers are available on YouTube 24/7. This is all good. But we still need to form individual bonds in the physical presence of people we care for and people who care about us. I fear too much emphasis on meditation as an exclusively interior practice does us a disservice. For as introspective as we become, we're going to have to go outside of ourselves to find many answers. We're going to have to rely on other people. We should know those people. Whether online or in person, we should deeply understand them as we offer up intimate details about ourselves.

If connectivity is helping you reach out to forge true, informed and caring connections, it's good. If it's a place to hide your truth or exclude others, it's not. While all the interior practices offered here can help you manage a mental illness, other people are going to factor into your success. That's why I think work, which I'll get to in a later chapter, is so important. Nothing builds connectivity like shared purpose.

I come back to meditation apps and online guidance. Aside from maybe a body scan, I think they're a terrible idea. Even groups who sit together and follow a guide are less than ideal. I sometimes lead such groups. People pay me good money to guide them through meditation. I don't do that as much anymore. I think it can be counterproductive when you're looking inside for clues to your condition to have someone yapping at you. The point, to steal a phrase from Brad Warner, is to sit down and shut up.

I remember a guided meditation I led. It was during a webinar for the International Bipolar Disorder Foundation. I led a standing meditation, an eye-opening experience in noticing things about something you've been doing your entire life that you never noticed before. (Some instructions are in the appendix.) But no one could come to this realization on their own because all I did was talk. There was no room for self-discovery or self-expression by the viewer. I committed the worst sin a meditation leader can commit. I told the people I was leading what to feel.

When I was a kid, I followed my grandmother into the occult. We did some pretty weird stuff, but she always warned me not to turn my thoughts over to anyone else while vulnerable or in spiritual practice. Ideas can be introduced that you would not choose in a stronger moment. Now I'm sure that the people who develop and sell meditation apps or guide group meditations aren't ostensibly into mind control, but they're still putting ideas in your head during moments of deep focus. Everyone has an agenda. Everyone thinks people should be a certain way, and this is especially true of those who work in behavioral fields, no matter how pure their motives. They have biases that will be introduced in their teaching or guidance. We're all guilty of that.

It's important to learn from masters. Today's connectivity gives us the opportunity to do that. Adopt their ideas, but don't hand yourself over to deep influence during your most vulnerable moments. That's not paranoid, that's pragmatic. Your answers are within you or in questions you generate that you can seek answers to later. Only you can discover the signs in your body and mind that signal that an episode of an affective disorder is imminent. Inevitably, only you, unless you're psychotic, can judge whether your thoughts are accurate or reflective or not. And you can't do that with the noise of someone talking at you, leading you off in some direction you may not profitably need or want to go while you're meditating. Learn first, then find connectivity and community in the trust of silence.

Secular Mindfulness

I write about and teach meditation with a very specific aim: to help people manage mental illness. It works. Still, I make no other vast claims about the practice. I avoid calling what I do 'mindfulness' because mindfulness speaks to a whole slew of now contradictory goals attributed to the same simple practice I recommend. My practice is born of that undertaken by the desert fathers and ancient Zen masters, and still practiced today by spiritual seekers across the world. It's also practiced by people like me, who use it for a very specific purpose instead of mystical experience or enlightenment. It's also practiced by the purveyors of secular mindfulness, who I think overpromise results for too little effort.

Meditation is hard work and, while often pleasant, it sometimes yields difficult experiences. It can relieve stress, or it can lead one to exaggerate stress. It's all about a person's relationship with their thoughts and the feelings in their body. I shiver when I hear secular mindfulness gurus promise all happy, happy. They seem to ignore the long history of struggle by meditation's masters. This tendency toward navigating struggle is what makes meditation so applicable to treating mental illness. But we must first acknowledge that much of what happens during meditation is a struggle. That's how we learn.

Years ago I sat as a student in an eight-week MBSR class. There was a woman sitting next to me who was disturbed about the process. During the second class she spoke up. She said she was an executive at a high stress firm, and she liked the pace. Type A-plus, she wanted to move fast and was afraid meditation would make her lose a step. She didn't want to be all calm and acquiescent and warm feeling. She wanted to clear her head and be creative. She wondered if she shouldn't be in the class. The teacher missed a tremendous teaching moment. Meditation could help her realize who she was, not change her into a person she didn't want to be. It could help her retain the best of herself and safely encounter what she was dissatisfied with. The beauty of the practice is that it offers almost exactly what anyone wants to get out of it. For crying out loud, this same MBSR program trained military snipers! But the teacher told her she was wrong. She should be all calm and laid back and hippie-like. She would be so much happier. The woman left at break and never came back.

I swore then that if I ever taught, it would be for people like her.

Much of what presents as mindfulness meditation these days is loosely based on Buddhist practices and comes with a progressive worldview attached. That's not OK for everybody. A typical secular mindfulness retreat will tangentially touch on some ideas from Buddhist sutras like the four noble truths. Briefly, these are 1) suffering is universal, 2) suffering is caused by an attachment to greed, hatred and delusion, 3) there is a way to end suffering, and 4) the way is the noble eightfold path. Three of the planks in the path are mindfulness, effort and concentration. That is pretty much what you get from many mindfulness gurus. That allows you to go inside of yourself and work on your own wellness. Complete view, resolve, speech, conduct and livelihood, the other five planks in the eightfold path, are pretty conservative values and look outward to our interactions with other people. They don't quite fit the self-focus of twenty-first-century secular mindfulness.

Mindfulness retreats often become Asian cultural appropriation carnivals complete with a little bit of yoga thrown in, vegetarian food and rice in a bowl, and the inevitable reading of something by the Sufi poet Rumi. They're not for everybody.

Absent is the rich history of contemplation in the Western tradition, but I think it's worth considering. Pick-and-choose Buddhism, presented with the limited knowledge of so many mindfulness adherents, can seem world negating, even nihilistic. Insistence on radical acceptance and karma borders on blaming the victim in cases of abuse and trauma. With everyone hell-bent on stress relief and self-improvement, little attention is often paid to the evil that lurks within us and positions itself against our mental health. Whether that evil is a thought construct or the devil himself, it's very real to a lot of very damaged people and needs to be recognized. Instead, oversimplified, the meditation instructions to "just let thoughts go" diminishes the impact that these thoughts can have on us when our mind is unhinged.

Judeo-Christian meditation practices approach this pull toward darkness head on. When I recited the Divine Office the focus of attention was the Psalms. I didn't have to dig too deep to find the anger and self-hate that mental illness had deposited within me. It was all over the Psalms. A prayer that asks God to crush the skulls of our enemies' children (Psalm 137) leaves little room for positive spin. But contemplating these verses helped. CS Lewis positions the Psalms as representative. The enemies we seek to smite are all within, and by exposing them we can move beyond and away from their influence and their negative control of our character, and the character of our thoughts and emotions. The Buddha went through similar exercises in his battles with the demon Mara, representative of all the demonic urges a person can hold inside. The Psalms and the sutras about Mara become poetic metaphors of our triumph over our worst impulses. This can help when dealing with the negative thoughts that flood us during the most desperate depressions and psychotic manias we face. Freudian critics will say that you can't pray mental illness away. But that's not the point of establishing archetypes to represent an internal struggle, and to meditate on them. Since meditation reveals so many of our thoughts as transitory and inaccurate, verses that speak of the struggle against these inaccuracies can help us see misleading thoughts for what they are. Defeatist and false.

If you can't pray mental illness away, I say you can't think it away either. Because it's not about thinking. Mental illness is as much a disorder of the body as it is of the mind. Gurus will speak of emptying the mind, and such a radical simplification of Zen will help you eliminate the unnecessary, but I'm willing to bet that reason is real and ideas matter. It's when your reason is broken that mental illness results. How do you think fighting a broken reason with more reason will go? Therapies and practices that extoll the benefits of thinking happy thoughts and present that as curative are suspect. Meditation presents you with only what is right before you and what you think about it, and how your body feels when you encounter it. It doesn't demand you change anything. It just asks you to notice before you try to adapt. Through meditation you can know what it means to be alive as you are right now; how you live and how life feels. Father Richard Rohr said it best when he said: "We don't think ourselves into new ways of being, we live ourselves into new ways of thinking."

People in the secular mindfulness world often define mindfulness as non-judgmental awareness of the present moment. But judging, while it can be defeating or unjust when it is in error, is necessary for survival. We judge what to eat and whether or not to walk down a dark alley. We judge ourselves and others, too, and that needs to be ferreted out and dealt with and judged either true or false. I guess you can practice non-judgment while you're meditating. That seems healthy enough. But is that the definition of mindfulness? This definition of mindfulness perpetuates the poor idea that mindfulness is something we do, often at set times within the bounds of a learned practice, then we get up and do something else. To be completely non-judgmental is to be open to injury and abuse, as well as to set oneself up to make poor decisions, or to put off decisions altogether until it's too late. When I'm meditating I'm often judging whether or not the feelings, thoughts and emotions I encounter are pointing to a coming episode of mania or depression or not. I don't want to miss that because of a questionable definition of mindfulness.

Buddhist teacher John Peacock defines mindfulness in a way I relate to and understand much better. He says mindfulness is the realization of where we are, and where we don't have to be. That will help us live with proper guidance, and we can practice that every waking minute.

I don't want to lose the pure beauty of practice. I think the commercialization of mindfulness risks that. The practice is too simple to be co-opted by the profit motive, and the stakes of living with mental illness are too high to be taken in by hucksterism. In always looking out and considering our place in the world as our meditation sessions extend into our daily lives, I think we can beat mental illness. There is no room for selfishness in what I propose. I've already lived through one 'me generation.' Years ago, I got wrapped up in an ultimately disappointing new age period that rejected traditional forms of wisdom for hocus pocus. Now all that is back in much of the mindfulness movement. I don't want to join the ascendant fads that have seized the meditation world. I'm set to lay out a method of meditation that can help predict and stave off the worst episodes of affective disorders. Then we can be selfless and join with others.

Chapter Five

When Not to Meditate

I was on a meditation retreat with James Austin, MD, a Zen teacher and researcher on Zen and the brain. I had an established practice of 30 minutes a day, but I had done very few retreats of more than a day or two. I told him that I was considering a long retreat, and I told him I have bipolar disorder. He said, "People with mental defects should not undergo long periods of meditation." I forgave him his choice of words, as he was in his nineties and different language was used when he first trained. I also decided to disregard his advice. I went on the long retreat and completely decompensated. The experience was full of the worst emotional pain that my illness had ever delivered. I survived it, and returned to meditating 30 minutes a day, and no more.

Years later, feeling more resilient and absent episodes of mixed mania and depression for a very long time, I tried it again. I had a challenging, but positive experience. It may not have been the wisest thing I ever did, but I thought that if I was to truly teach, I had to push myself to discover limits that any of my students might face. In this book I'm not advocating long retreats or long sessions of meditation. I recommend an established daily practice of 20 minutes to a half-hour. I feel that can benefit almost anyone. Most of the time.

Meditation can help you get through an episode of anxiety, depression or mania by betraying the thoughts that fuel such episodes as false, by giving you some calm space to survey your situation and predict your moods, and by revealing some ideas on how to intervene. But only if you have an established practice. If you have not meditated regularly, or at all, and you're in a period of depressed ideation, impulsive mania or torturous anxiety, don't start now. You'll just sit there agitated and ruminate and your condition will likely get worse. Seek help elsewhere. Begin practice during a stable period.

When I first considered meditation, my mind was still troubled by an episode of mania that resulted in a hospitalization. Anxious rumination unsettled my thoughts, and to sit quietly observing such thoughts likely would have pushed me over the edge. I read the Psalms instead. Today, with a well-established practice, focused attention helps me navigate and overcome such difficult periods. But as a beginner, silent practice right then would have been dangerous.

It's best to begin meditating during a period of relative stability. If one is depressed and contemplating suicide, a new meditation practice will not help at all. If a terribly depressed person sits with those thoughts, things are only likely to get worse. After establishing a strong practice, the same focus at the same time may help a person release such thoughts and be well. But not as a beginner.

Anxiety is a similar situation. The beauty in using meditation to manage anxiety is the revelation of self-defeating thoughts. As I stated before, we've all thought, *I'm so anxious I could die!* Meditating on this reveals that you don't die. Thoughts fuel the anxiety, and if you can see the thoughts as erroneous and let them go the anxiety inflamed by them will pass, too. But not until you've practiced long enough to face and release thoughts with confidence. As a beginner, the rumination will only further convince you that, yes, the anxiety will kill you.

Most studies that prove the beneficial effects of meditation have their subjects meditate for 20 minutes a day for four to eight weeks before lasting positive results are established. (Of course, you have to keep practicing for the positive effects to remain.) It takes about that long to learn how to successfully sit and notice the changes in and around you. It takes about that long to learn how to release thoughts that don't make sense. It takes a bit longer to predict episodes by noting signals in your body, emotions and mind. If you haven't put in a few weeks of practice when you're well, don't meditate when things are too challenging to endure. Call a hotline or reach out to a loved one or doctor instead.

Today many teachers with little depth of understanding of the challenges meditators can face are leading students into practices that, while often very positive and relaxing, can lead a troubled mind into very dangerous places. Just as a poorly trained yoga teacher can push a student to physical injury, an insensitive meditation teacher can introduce practices that add dangerous rumination to the challenges one may face. This can be especially damaging to people with serious mental illness.

Even expert, world-famous teachers have students who have come apart, some requiring hospitalization. Recent research published in PLOS One indicates that 25% of people who have meditated for at least two months have reported a particularly unpleasant psychological experience, such as anxiety, fear, distorted emotions or thoughts, or an altered sense of self or the world while meditating.[2] Meditators who have practiced for years, or long periods of time during each sitting, had an even higher occurrence of challenging experiences.

Those most at risk include those who suffer from high levels of repetitive negative thinking, as do many with serious mental illness. This is not to say that meditation cannot benefit those with serious mental illness. It saved my life from the ruin of bipolar disorder. It just needs to be entered into carefully, and with support.

Difficulty while meditating should really come as no surprise. Christian mystics have been writing about it for millennia as the dark night of the soul, and the Buddha spoke of his struggles with Mara, representative of all the negativity the mind can present the meditator. Most faith traditions recognize that suffering is universal, so of course people will suffer during meditation.

This isn't necessarily a bad thing. Meditation, as detailed in these faith traditions, affords the meditator the opportunity to successfully approach difficult emotions and thoughts. As Dr Peter Tse notes, pain and mental anguish serve a purpose: to motivate us to find a way out of our present state of misery. However, many meditation teachers are ignorant of this history and see only the positive in the practice. The positive is surely there, but for a person with a serious mental illness the path to positive results may be fraught with the deep horrors of the mind.

We must be careful of promoting therapies as having blanket, unquestioned benefit for everyone. I fear we over-promote mindfulness meditation as too easy, and people who have bad experiences are left only to blame themselves for being "bad meditators," getting little follow-up support even from some nationally recognized programs. Those who enter into meditation through apps or online guidance get no support at all.

Anything people sell you as a cure-all should be met with skepticism. Yes, meditation can yield very positive results to most who undertake it—including most people with mental illness. But a measure of caution is always warranted. If it all sounds too easy, it likely doesn't work. If when undertaken it seems so difficult as to be dangerous, maybe one should stop.

This may sound like the whole idea of meditation is pointless. Why practice something that can do harm? Well, medicine given at the wrong time or in the wrong dose can do harm, too. The point is to practice meditation under fairly controlled conditions; to learn the right way and the right amount of time for you to practice as you begin to move into this form of focused attention. If all you get out of it is the ability to predict mood changes, that's enough to be life changing.

If meditation continues to take you to bad places but you

feel compelled to tough it out and make it work, don't force classic, seated meditation to be a positive experience when it has betrayed itself as harmful to you. Try a practice like Lectio Divina, or divine reading, practiced by monks and oblates who follow the rule of St Benedict. It can keep your mind more engaged than distracted, and the reading you choose can lead you to great improvement in your experience with mental illness and life.

In Lectio Divina you choose something profound or inspirational to read. Traditionally, sacred texts like the Psalms have been used, but I often read things that range from ancient Chinese poetry to Shakespeare's sonnets. Still, the Psalms remain my favorite. Simply pick a short passage of the literature and read it over and over until some even shorter phrase or a word jumps out at you. Then repeat that word or very short phrase several times. When fully focused on the word or phrase, stop repeating it and silence the mind as best you can. Notice new thoughts that form and contemplate the ideas the reading sparks in you. Or notice that nothing of interest happens at all. Take what comes, and when you lose the train of thought entirely return your focus to the longer piece of writing you chose and begin again.

This method of focused attention touches on embracing thoughts, unlike classic, seated meditation, and it will sometimes yield deep insight into events surrounding you or emotions deep within you that signal mood changes that must be noticed. As with other practices, this exposure of brewing transition can lead you to safely intervene and avoid troubling episodes of anxiety, depression or mania. If not, it can still reveal some fascinating inspiration you hadn't noticed before in something important you've read. Either way, you can experience the benefits of focused attention while avoiding the troubling rumination that just sitting in long periods of silence can bring.

Another means of entering the focused attention of

meditative practice without suffering long periods of absolute silence is to say the rosary. The rosary, or other prayer beads that offer introspection and respect for tradition, enables one to achieve a spiritual, centered state of disciplined focus through a sacred practice not dumbed down or devoid of meaning as so many modern secular practices are; practices starved of original heartfelt intent by new age gurus who present such methods divorced from the strict community-based spiritual power they once offered, and still do, to people of faith. If you have a strong belief in God, don't set it aside while seeking the benefits of contemplation, especially contemplation aimed at measuring the influence of mental illness on your life and soul.

You can still go deep within the body to learn about and predict oncoming episodes of anxiety, depression or mania during deep, repeated, meaningful prayer.

Self-Absorption Leads to Isolation

Mental illness is a terribly lonely place. One so stricken often feels isolated and misunderstood. The heart aches and the body gets physically sick. Alienation is a reality for many with affective disorders. The word "alienation" comes from a very old root that meant to be separated from one's God. Some time spent contemplating what we believe sets us apart from others or what makes us different, and feeling the sensations these ideas bring, can both challenge and enlighten us. All it takes is incredible humility and honesty to carefully explore what illness has done, and continues to do, to our connection with other people, our bodies and our sense of spirituality:

- Where lies our responsibility to others, and our responsibility to the ethics, morals and/or God we seek to follow to become well?
- Can we forgive ourselves for any ill will we wish on ourselves or others?

- Can we reconcile with those we have cut off in our struggle with a disfigured mind?
- What work do we need to do to change society and its influence on the illness and ill will people feel?

That which holds us apart from others adds to any sense of isolation and clouds any chance of self-discovery. We live in community. We are joined in a very deep sense to other people. Even at our most despondent we are never truly alone. Maybe the self-absorption of some forms of therapy is a bad idea, for there is always someone available to us: a lost family member, a struggling friend, God, a peer group, a connection made online or someone from the clergy. Alienation can be overcome, but to defeat it we must reach out.

Isolationist practices, as meditation is conducted by some, can be damaging. Ideas that make us responsible for healing the stress within us without confronting the stressors that contribute to our illness are too passive, and soul-crushing, to be effective. The point of meditation is not to be alone pulling all your weight yourself, and if meditation breeds a sense of self-blame or failure within you, you're definitely receiving some bad information about it.

Today mindfulness is taught with a near-complete focus on the self and as a method of self-improvement. Teachers instruct us that through this self-focus we can better ourselves and overcome our own suffering. But this elevation of the self to a place of responsibility for how we suffer, and how we feel, this reinforcement of our ideal of the individual as the agent of their own well-being that predominates in our culture, and most mindfulness instruction, may be a prime cause of suffering. Self-absorption only drowns us in more pain. In fact, in the ancient and medieval traditions from which mindfulness and most meditation methods spring, there is near-universal agreement that suffering comes from selfish desire. Too much focus on the self, too much insistence on how we, as individuals, suffer, can paradoxically lead to even more suffering as we place ourselves first and emphasize care for ourselves over care for others as the corrective for our ills.

This poses a real problem for those of us with mental illness. Mental illness, and the quest to overcome mental illness, can lead to self-absorption as we lose ourselves in our own misery and forget about the society in which we live. We forget about our responsibility to live with charity, conviction and productivity. It's OK to be unhappy if you see problems that need to be addressed in our culture, problems that inflame our disease, if that unhappiness motivates you to work to change things for the better. Good may come for many more people than just yourself. Mindfulness practices that keep us looking inward for answers can serve to reinforce the pain and anguish we construct in our mind, often with tools handed to us by society and its pervasive idea that all we have to do is change our mind and all will be OK. Meditation, done wrong, can isolate us from the world around us. We miss the joy of connectivity and the wealth of beauty found about us when we suffer alone.

Mental illness is positioned as a disease of the self, and it's true that only we, as individuals, can experience our own minds. But we exist in concert with others, and any individual's disease must also be accepted as a disease that affects our influence on, and the influence of, others. We must consider the possibility that all of this focus on us as separate beings with individual solutions, this complete obsession with the self, is a contributing factor to the explosion of mental illness we face in our culture.

We're told that we are exceptional as whole individuals, but most of us are pretty mediocre at most of what we do. We get by and possibly do one or two things well, but when held up to the bright lights in the world we dim. And yet, we strive for someone else's ideal. However, in our influence on those around us, in our participation in our families and our community, we can be exceptional. While we engage in social media that reinforces our belief that the latest thought we had is original and profound, or that what we're doing right now is of significant interest to others, we miss the fact that it's our quiet influence, our gently passing through the lives of others, that changes the world. And changes us.

Instead, we join the cult of the individual and overemphasize our own well-being while, in fact, through that overemphasis on our own good we make ourselves sick. Sure, there are things to get up and protest. Just not in favor of selfish things. We heal through connection, not removing ourselves from society and focusing only on ourselves. That's probably why we experience mental illness, beyond the influence of biochemistry and neurotransmitters, in the first place.

We must consider that the more special we think we are, the more capable we feel of achieving great things completely on our own, the more vulnerable we are to collapsing if any small failing proves us wrong or if we can't find the energy to follow through. To focus exclusively on ourselves and our own happiness can ultimately exaggerate those failings. Connectivity, a focus on how we influence others and how they influence us, positively and negatively, will in fact heal our broken minds more than any practice that sets the self apart from the community.

So if meditation becomes a selfish practice with a goal of making us better without regard for others, it is better left undone. Get out and do something. Self-care and self-improvement can only be achieved by focusing completely on our impact on others. Sure, while meditating we follow thoughts and seek to be well and predict mood changes, but mental health requires that we let go of our self-absorption and return to the world in which we may feel uncomfortable. If meditation helps you realize and accomplish that, go for it. If it re-emphasizes yourself as an isolated individual entirely responsible for your own failings, as well as your successes, try a practice that is more outward looking—something that doesn't leave you alone in your room, scouring your mind for ways that you are at fault for all of your suffering. Get outside. Reach out to others. Stop obsessing on and blaming yourself.

It's Not Always Going to Be Pleasant

As you reach out and look inward, give yourself the time to learn. Always measure how you physically feel about things, both things that make you happy and things that piss you off. Self-knowledge does not hit you in the head with one big stroke of enlightenment. You have to work at it, and always practice. Your muscle memory, the feelings triggered deep within by the experience of discovery, is crucial to this exploration and revelation.

As you investigate yourself and your world, keep the body and what it's feeling of equal importance to what's going on in your mind. To contemplate what you encounter in what comes up in the mind and body is key. If meditation induces anxiety or reinforces depression or grandiosity and impulsiveness, consider instead practices that get you out among others. This is more active than sitting and noticing things, and may be safer to explore for those too challenged by classic, seated, silent meditation. Of course, if in any practice you encounter deep-seated emotional issues you can't resolve yourself, or if you're dealing with abuse or trauma, reach out to close confidants and professionals. The suffering from these events is from severe injustice, not selfish desire. You will need outside help to resolve it. Anger and self-destructive impulses are usually founded on false beliefs or ideas not fully formed. You need the space to self-correct and to confront injustice. But if your ability to admit and own up to your own failings or inconsistencies during meditation is limited, you must abandon the idea of self-directed therapy through contemplation and seek help with someone you can trust. The beauty of the introspection enabled through active contemplation is that it can help with this process as well.

So whereas meditation will give you the clarity of mind and calm any internal chatter to help you notice oncoming episodes, outward-directed contemplation and insight can also help along any efforts to improve your relationship with the disease that afflicts you, and to begin the process of healing that will help you live a well-managed life.

There are other more active alternative forms of meditation you can practice. One, walking meditation, we'll cover in the section on movement. We'll get to the idea of art or journaling in the section on meaningful work.

Be careful of meditating to achieve enlightenment. Enlightenment is a noble goal, but let's be practical. We're trying to live with mental illness and contribute positively to the world. There are many paths to get there. In introducing some alternative practices and giving you the option to pass on classic, seated meditation, I offer here one last thought on practice.

One of the main reasons I practice, as I've tried to illustrate, is to predict oncoming episodes. It took a long time for me to learn how to do that. I developed the techniques and built confidence in my practice while the symptoms of my bipolar disorder were very distant. Affective disorders are usually episodic. There is often time to learn to practice before or between serious episodes.

Once you've got the knack for it, meditation will help you when things go wrong. But it's not all good as some well-known teachers have promised. The mind and body can present you with some pretty uncomfortable situations as you sit and focus on an object of attention, and subsequently on thoughts and feelings. Some things are easier to let go of than others. Resolving abuse or trauma is going to take more than meditation, especially when teachers tell you that your thoughts are the problem, not what has happened to you. Nothing could be further from the truth. Accepting your thoughts as the reason for your despair is the opposite of changing things for the better. Your thoughts and experience are inextricably linked, and you can't dismiss one and focus exclusively on the other. You also can't heal from abuse while considering forms of moral relativism. Some things are just wrong. Too much emphasis on acceptance and too much culpability placed on your thoughts about events may not be the way to heal. This idea that underlies much Eastern thought that influences secular meditation practices as misinterpreted by many Western teachers presents a system without escape that blames the victim for their own suffering. The idea of karma as presented by many ill-equipped teachers in the West perpetuates this false belief. If you were a victim of abuse, it was not your fault, and no system of moral relativism or radical acceptance, or karma, should in any way make you feel culpable for evil things that happened to you. Contemplation on truth and responsibility will clearly reveal this. While you don't want to blame other people or some system for every bad thing that happens to you, in cases of physical or severe emotional abuse or trauma or profound social injustice you're off the hook.

Remember, meditation is not always going to be pleasant, and you're going to have to go far beyond it to resolve, or heal, some things that have happened in your life. You need other people, and great faith in some ideal.

Begin to practice meditation when things are smoother and internal feelings are more secure. If medication and therapy add stability to your life, use that time to add meditation to your list of coping skills. Build up to a resilient practice that can withstand a barrage of difficult thoughts. If meditation is challenging, don't quit. You'll get through the difficulty. But if it's damaging, if the thoughts or sensations you encounter while meditating exacerbate all that is wrong, stop. Take a walk, work on a puzzle, trust a friend. Work for a cause. Call for help. Find another therapy like the ones I'll outline next. Focused attention can still help; just maybe not classic, seated meditation. This is when movement and meaningful work can be beneficial and, in some cases, even superior to seated, silent meditation.

Section Two

Movement

The heavens themselves run continually round, the sun rises and sets, the moon increases and decreases, stars and planets keep their constant motions, the air is still tossed by the winds, the waters ebb and flow, to their conservation no doubt, to teach us that we should ever be in action.
—Robert Burton, *The Anatomy of Melancholy*, 1621

Chapter Six

Why Move?

Meditation is not for everyone. One research paper I read stated that of all the people who try it, only 22% continue to meditate daily after only two months.[3] This may be because expectations are not being met, and I make the case that the expectations set by many of meditation's proponents are preposterous, or that meditation, for many of those who don't stick with it, is not a pleasant experience. I argue that it's not meant to be, you just experience however you feel that day, but I concede that a practice someone takes up to relieve stress should not add stress to their life, and an activity promoted to help minimize suffering should not make one suffer more, as in the case of dangerous rumination or perseveration that may be encountered during meditation, especially in people with severe anxiety or suicidal depression. Those who meditate for religious or spiritual purpose tend to push through this, and many others find the practice beneficial for the reasons outlined in Section One, but obviously there must be some other ways to focus the attention and develop the ability to predict, prevent and manage episodes of anxiety, depression and mania.

Movement is one.

Movement can be approached without expectations other than to improve one's level of fitness. There are so many ways to move that inevitably each person can find one that suits them. Movement can also act as a sort of meditation. One's full attention can turn to meet the body in motion. The body is a tremendous point of focus, and as it moves one can practice with all of the feelings expressed throughout the core and limbs. Movement has benefits beyond focusing the attention, too. It improves physical and mental health and can combat the long list of diseases that are comorbid with mental illness. Movement also instills some sense of control and self-confidence.

While the methods presented in this book help ameliorate mood changes, mood changes still come. Many people with affective disorders are troubled by the sense of how little control they seem to have over where their minds may take them, but we must recall that the mind usually follows the body. Movement practices help us moderate difficult moods. Still, it's hard to get out of our heads and get over this sense of losing control every time our moods swing to an uncomfortable place. In this pining for control we must recognize that one thing we do have control over is our physical fitness, and this is a great place to begin to influence our moods and our minds.

Some may find the words "movement practice" annoying. It does sound a little pompous. Why not just call it exercise? Well, exercise is a big part of what I practice, but I practice it with the added intention of moderating my moods. This requires that I place intense focus on my exercise regimen, and some forms of exercise lend themselves better to this sort of focus than others.

Rhythmic exercise has been shown to temper mood swings and it offers a great sense of stress relief. These exercises include walking, running and swimming. It's easy to see how a person can bring their full focus to these activities and rest their mind in the physical movement of the body and the terrain or surface covered. Research illustrates that these exercises are especially effective in minimizing episodes of mania. Depression and anxiety seem to benefit from almost all forms of exercise. We're always moving. Not all movement, such as walking to the car or through the grocery store, is what we would call exercise. Yet we can practice with all movement.

It's natural to move, and necessary. There are few things more beautiful than a person in full stride, whether quickly pacing down the street or reaching for a long pass in the endzone. Nothing I've seen is more joyful than kids dancing and splashing in a spray ground, and to wrestle and run with my dogs takes me far from any troubles that bother me. In these acts we can each fire the mind into a place of consistency as we move. We can do this by placing our attention entirely on the body and not getting caught up in the endless loop of rumination over false and defeating thoughts on which our minds tend to fixate.

Our attitude toward exercise says a lot about how we feel about ourselves. Whether or not we move regularly may signify our motivation to be well, or it may illustrate where we believe our mental illness truly resides. Mental illness is in itself a limiting diagnosis. It forces us within. It implies that we can best be treated through medicine that impacts our brain, which is where most of us locate our minds. The medication is often crucial to our wellness, but there is so much more to pay attention to than our neurochemistry.

Remember that in ancient traditions no distinction was made between the mind and the body. In treating mental illness we must treat both together. If episodes of difficulty in affective disorders begin as physical expressions, which I believe they do, to move is imperative to positively experience and overcome these episodes. We must not ignore our bodies. Healthy body/ healthy mind may seem like a cliché we print on posters for nutrition classes, but it succinctly illustrates what we all must learn in order to feel better and take the necessary steps toward wellness. The mind and body are inseparable.

This linkage can have its downside. When the mind is sick, so, often, is the body. This joint difficulty is expressed as comorbidity, or medical conditions that occur together.

Comorbidity

Movement never came easy to me. All my life, I'd rather sit and read. There'd be times when mania would take me deep into an obsession with sport, and I'd buy sneakers and track jackets and exercise every moment, lost in a frenzy of fitness. But mania would just as likely drive me to drink. The impulse to move would pass, and with it the drive to get in shape. My time spent running would return to the written page and great big ideas. It took a level mood and the aches that come with age to realize that moving around as much as I can is a great big idea, too.

A lot of movement is forced on me. We live in a neighborhood just off Center City in Philadelphia where cars are a terrible inconvenience. So I walk everywhere. Miles a day. The walking and a short routine of calisthenics each morning keep me fit enough, so I enjoy the benefits of being active. The walking and the light exercise combine with eating well to keep the worst of the diseases that are comorbid with bipolar disorder from making me ill. This is quite an accomplishment, as people with bipolar disorder are in notoriously bad shape. Nearly 70% are overweight.[4]

People with affective disorders tend to die young. The average age of death for someone with bipolar disorder is 56. Suicide skews the number, of course, as 15% of people with bipolar disorder die of suicide, but most people with mental illness suffer from a slew of physical diseases that commonly occur with affective disorders.[5] Mental illness can make life hell, but these physical diseases are the ones that kill.

Because of the extra weight that most people with affective disorders carry, diabetes, hypertension and heart disease are the most common comorbid conditions. Pulmonary disease strikes many as well, which is no surprise given that over 60% of people with severe mood disorders smoke. Excessive alcohol use leads to liver disease in this population, also. Yet these diseases, along with cancer, kill most people in the general population, too, as they do people with mental illness. However, a few diseases strike people with affective disorders at unusually high rates.

People with mood disorders show significantly more cases of gastrointestinal disease and musculoskeletal abnormalities.

People with anxiety also experience gastrointestinal disease at high rates, and have a unique tendency toward psoriasis. Headaches, especially migraines, are also more common in people with affective disorders. These illnesses may not sound as life-threatening as some of the other comorbidities, but they can make life awful.

People aren't kidding when they say you feel it in your gut. For many of us, this is where episodes will show up in the body first, and GI distress can be a sure early signal that an episode of anxiety or mood change is imminent. Whether in meditation or movement, pay special attention to the feelings in your abdomen. The mind–gut connection is well established in medicine. The gut is filled with receptors for the neurotransmitters that influence mood. Explorations in mind–body medicine seem to take us right to our mid-section. The stress that bedevils us and results in these gut problems can be relieved with movement practice.

I suffered from serious GI distress for years before I was finally diagnosed with celiac disease. It should be no surprise to learn that celiac disease, an autoimmune inflammation disorder, is 17 times more common in people with bipolar disorder than it is in the general population.[6] Much research is being done into the influence of inflammation on affective disorders, and evidence points to the contribution of autoimmune factors on the development of mood disorders. We're early to this research, but it won't be surprising to learn more about the links between inflammation and diseases of the mind.

I haven't escaped the musculoskeletal comorbidities either. I have terrible arthritis (autoimmune inflammation again) and a very early case of osteoporosis. The calcium-leaching effects of the celiac disease and years of taking anticonvulsants for bipolar disorder may contribute to this, but my doctor is unwilling to commit. Whatever the reason, these musculoskeletal troubles are not unique to me. They're common in people with mood disorders. Depression is associated with a 53% increase in bone fracture, and people with affective disorders have over 7% less bone density than others.[7] Weight-bearing exercise will help us improve and increase bone density.

For those with anxiety, the uncertainty-fueled influence of stress is an understandable explanation for the proliferation of GI problems and psoriasis. Thyroid difficulties also commonly appear in people with generalized anxiety disorder and bipolar disorder.

It's pointless to try to determine if the mental illness causes the physical illness, or vice versa. The diseases occur together, so a flare-up in one is likely to signal difficulty with its comorbid counterpart. The best way to health and disease management is to take care of yourself with enough sleep, a healthy, varied diet, practices to relieve stress, few intoxicants, and regular exercise. The exercise, while good in its own merit, can be used not only as a practice to manage health and illness, but also as a practice in focused attention akin to meditation. By bringing your full attention onto your body while moving, feeling your pulse quicken and your breath become more deliberate, you can develop a practice just as effective as meditation to anticipate oncoming episodes of anxiety and disturbing changes in mood. When you move, your body sings. All you have to do is listen to it.

Movement may be the most cost-effective way to improve your health and your quality of life. It will counter the risk of chronic comorbid diseases that often result from changes in behavior, a sedentary lifestyle, or medication side effects. It can also boost your self-esteem and your memory, your mood and your motivation. Exercising or participating in sports with others will positively impact self-confidence and your sense of social interaction, and movement will help improve physiologic reactivity to stress—it will help calm you down.

The Body Is Not a Problem to Be Overcome

Aerobic exercise reduces anxiety and depression in all its forms. People who suffer from mania, though, have to be a little more selective of the movement practice they choose. Exercise-induced mania is a thing.

Here we have a chicken-and-the-egg problem. Does the intense exercise cause the mania or does mania cause one to engage in intense exercise? The only times I've participated in high-intensity interval training were times when my mood was elevated and my impulse control was low. I don't know if the psychiatric symptoms or the physical energy came first, but I do know that the co-occurrence of energy-burst-filled exercise with the grandiosity of mania often led not to invincibility but to injury. In this I am not alone. The link between intense exercise and mania has been documented in research.

Rhythmic exercises seem to be the answer. Intermittent bursts of expended energy during exercise is what co-occurs with exercise-induced mania. Exercise for people with bipolar disorder 1, which results in frequent episodes of mania, can be intense, if that intensity is maintained and consistent as it is in walking, running or swimming. Bursts of power may not best serve those who tend toward mania, but this is no reason to avoid exercise. Plenty of movement practices are available to try. One, or a few, will inevitably work well and lead to more predictable, and more level, moods.

Once you have found a practice you can stick to, one you look forward to, one that's not boring, and do it at least three days a week for 30 minutes each day (you can break it into 10-minute intervals), the health benefits will pay great dividends. Of course, if you want to make movement a much bigger part of your life you can. There are movement cultures like martial arts, surfing, rock climbing, street dancing and parkour that have their own codes and tend to be very inclusive, open to new members, and encourage practitioners with very positive standards and messages. Whatever you do, if you just get up and move you'll find the following things happen:

- Improved sleep
- Better endurance
- Stress relief
- Improvement in mood
- Increased interest in sex
- Increased energy and stamina
- Reduced tiredness/increased mental alertness
- Weight reduction
- Reduced cholesterol levels
- Improved cardiovascular fitness

You don't need a gym membership, or fancy clothes and equipment. In fact, I'll make the case that you're better off without these things. If you exercise you will feel better, measure your moods more accurately, and be able to intervene when the body speaks and tells you the mind has taken a turn into a stagnant or a fiery spot. You just have to move and pay attention.

Too many of us are uncomfortable in our bodies. Whether it's our culture's relentless focus on how we look or medicine's obsessive concentration on illness and decay, many see the body as a problem to be overcome. We've made mere movement difficult and full of baggage. We don't know our own bodies. It's like we're trapped in an intricate puzzle and haven't the slightest idea where all the pieces should go. But all the pieces are already in place. We exist not inside of, but fully in concert with, our bodies. We shouldn't just live from the neck up. To think that the word "me" speaks more of our thoughts and opinions than our knees and our elbows is silly. We are physical and we are complete. The puzzle is already solved.

Of course we can continue to move the pieces around—

change the way we feel, change the way we think. We're always moving. We're never still. As we move through life, life moves through us. As we discover when we meditate and create when we work, when we move we're a work in progress. As we move we influence the result.

Chapter Seven

The Benefits of Movement

I feel better when I move. Simple movements: walking; a basic stretch; chasing my daughter or the dogs across the baseball diamond. Although I treasure the still quiet of seated meditation, when I'm out and about, moving, I feel most alive. Where we live I can walk everywhere. Just about a dozen blocks to the grocery store and the same trip back, carrying bags. If the journey is a lot further I'll take the bus, but I always get off early and walk the last bit.

Movement brings with it a host of health benefits. If you're used to moving and need to get around you're unlikely to overeat or drink too much. Those things make you bloated and distorted and trapped in place. Movement shouldn't be uncomfortable, although it will sometimes be challenging and difficult. It should inspire you and charge you with purpose. Ideas seem to come better when I move, and moving briskly gets the pulse up and excites the nerves in a very positive way.

Also, movement can be a tremendous way to meditate.

When I teach meditation I try to incorporate both standing and walking meditation into my class. When the body rises from the seated position thoughts change, as do the sensations in the body. A new pattern of awareness opens up and the mind, preoccupied with keeping the body upright and moving, often calms in a way less attainable when completely still and left with only what our minds present us instead of activity.

Anxiety or a mood change often throws me right onto the couch or sends me to nervously wear a path on the carpet, pacing back and forth. Both responses are a sort of inertia that must be broken if a level state of mind is to be restored. The answer is always to go to the body; to break the inertia of a troubled mind by bringing your full focus to physical sensations. Movement helps. It implies getting somewhere, accomplishing something with the body. If I can break away from the lethargy of the sofa or the tight, redundant pattern of prowling one room, I can see myself getting better and feel my mood improve.

This type of movement doesn't have to be a fancy workout, either. In fact, it's better if it's not. Pushing a vacuum, painting a wall or running through a forest will always yield better results than circuit training in a noisy gym. The simpler the practice, the better. Movement activities will make you feel good. Find a few. Try a few. Move.

Effects on Mood

Diet and sleep are key harbingers of health, yet exercise may rule largest as it has mood-stabilizing benefits as well as a positive impact on physical health and, in this way, diet and sleep. Regular movement will increase metabolism and decrease the resting heart rate. It will help control blood sugar, regulate blood pressure, and lower negative levels of stress. Exercise is something of a panacea, and regular movement practice will lead to better health in a person with mental illness with results as effective as medicine and talk therapy. The benefits of movement cannot be overstated.

Besides all the obvious physical health benefits, movement can have a tremendous impact on mood. It's hard to be brooding or preoccupied with woe when you're huffing for air over the last few hundred meters of a 5k intent on a personal best. There's brain chemistry involved. The rush of endorphins that results from physical effort can lift the most troubled soul.

Aerobic exercise, the result of vigorous movement, elevates the mood. Sustained effort that keeps the heart rate up can deliver benefits to all the systems of the body. Movement brings you to health as it takes you from illness to wellness. This makes me consider the word "movement." "To move" is a verb that means to proceed toward a certain state or condition. The idea is that through locomotion you get from one place to another. This can be from a bad place to a good place. You travel. You progress.

Poor moods restrict you from moving. Idioms like "stuck in a rut" that we use to describe glumness and inactivity illustrate just how crucial movement is to keeping our moods positive, or at least progressively better. As we move we are presented with new stimuli, new things for our senses to experience as our pulses elevate, sweat beads on our skin, and the landscape changes. Good moods move us forward. Bad moods hold us back. A bad mood can improve when you're going somewhere with a task to reach some goal, be it the day's ten thousandth step, 80% of VO2 max, or to see the cardinal's nest in the tree in the glide off the horse path.

Regular exercise, defined as 30 minutes a day, 3–5 days per week, reduces anxiety, depression and negative mood. It helps to subdue responses from both the sympathetic nervous system (responsible for the fight-or-flight reaction) and the hypothalamic–pituitary–adrenal axis, the hormonal feedback system that reacts to stress. It works like an antidepressant, increasing levels of neurotransmitters like serotonin and norepinephrine in the brain, thus boosting mood. Moderate exercise will prompt the release of endorphins, naturally occurring opioids produced by the body, and will enhance someone's sense of self-efficacy, the belief that they are capable of accomplishing their goals. This helps to minimize anxiety. Movement has a positive impact on memory and reduces distraction. It can even increase self-esteem and make a person more eager to engage in social interaction.

The American Psychiatric Association describes the exercise effect on anxiety. Episodes of anxiety and exercise share heavy perspiration and elevated heart rate as symptoms. Experiencing these physiological changes while exercising, and establishing positive associations with these bodily experiences, make it less likely that a person's experience with anxiety will escalate into a panic attack. Movement practice trains the person to associate these symptoms with safety instead of danger.

Research has followed people who exercise and people who take medication for 16 weeks to see how different therapies impact depression remission. 45% of the people who only practiced supervised exercise remained in remission. 40% who did home-based exercise remained in remission. Of the people on medication only, 47% remained in remission. In the placebo group 31% stayed in remission.[8] Exercise had nearly the same depression-fighting effect as medication.

In people with bipolar disorder regular exercise leads to lower psychiatric comorbidities such as anxiety or psychosis, and fewer depressive episodes.

Most of the research cited measured people who undertook aerobic exercise, which appears to have superior mood-stabilizing effects to anaerobic exercise such as weightlifting, although the few studies that have looked at anaerobic exercise's impact on affective disorders are returning promising results.

Movement and Focused Attention

Movement provides compelling opportunities to bring one's full attention onto the body and anticipate the unexpected mood changes that trip up people with affective disorders. As in meditation, one can grab the attention and place it right on a chosen point of focus. In movement, the body becomes an even more significant focal point than the breath, enabling the practitioner to measure their full range of physiological sensations and better predict new episodes of anxiety, depression or mania.

When the mind is occupied with things like balance, motion, time and space, many people find it easier to release persistent thoughts by using movement practice as a form of meditation.

The most obvious activity that presents itself for this sort of practice is yoga, and in fact yoga was originally practiced to prepare the body for long periods of seated meditation. Unfortunately, yoga has taken on an exclusive culture, much like the mindfulness industry, that layers on everything from consumerism to progressive political views to new age spirituality that many people do not find appealing. Most yoga studios are not welcoming places for overweight, sedentary people with mental illness. Exceptions do exist, and if you find one that suits you dive in, but they are difficult to come by.

Fortunately, yoga is not the only opportune practice for moving meditation. Anything from pull-ups in the playground to dancing to polyrhythmic music will do.

It helps to begin with very slow, basic movements to train the attention to settle on the place in your body where you're most conscious of the movement. You can start standing still with your focus on the breath, but as you begin to move allow your attention to open up into the full awareness of the body moving. Then, when prepared, narrow the attention down to the part of your body you choose to focus on as you move. This may be your bicep while you crank out curls or your full body in motion in cross-country skiing. Any exercise presents well for this practice.

As you practice bring your attention to that point in your body where you most feel the motion. As with seated meditation, dismiss thoughts that distract you from this moment. Don't talk to yourself, don't belittle or praise yourself. With humility merge your mind, through focus, with your body. Athletes tell of a runner's high or a flow state in which their full awareness is simply the body moving, completing its task as if without effort. Here the mind clears and it completely rejoins the body. While you just can't will this state, in moving meditation you can experience it at any level of skill.

Physicality may surprise you as a meditation practice.

Isn't meditation supposed to be quiet and still? Remember, meditation at its most basic is about noticing what's going on within and around you. Purposeful movement can provide this just as well as sitting with your legs crossed. One practice that makes for a transition from seated meditation to a combination of seated and moving practice can also be taken as training for people who only want to engage in movement practice and skip seated practice entirely. Try the following:

Exercise vigorously for a few minutes to get the heart rate up. Jumping jacks are great for this. While jumping, focus on the flailing of your arms, the hard contact your feet make with the floor, and the quickening of your breath. When well exercised and feeling a bit worn out stop and stand still or sit. Feel the body begin to relax and bring the attention into the chest. You'll feel your breath heaving and your heart pounding. Remain still for as long as it takes your breath and heart rate to return to rest. Keep the focus in your chest as you feel the heart and the breath slow down. If distracted by thoughts, return your attention to your chest. When fully relaxed, and this may take more than a few minutes, bring your attention to your full body for a moment, feel your full self in its resting state, then return to exercise or end this session of practice. A variation on this practice is simply standing still, which you'll be surprised to learn meets the criteria for movement practice. This practice is described in the appendix.

Once you've learned from this practice to bring your full attention to the body, you can practice more intently while you move. Unless you're practicing movement that requires music, like dancing, exercise in silence. Run or walk without earbuds, move in your house without streaming media. Minimize distractions to assist your full focus to come to your body as you move.

From here it is a natural step to feel a unification of the body and the mind as they return to their active state of being one.

With your itemized list of physical symptoms of oncoming episodes, you can more easily sense these changes in your body and act to prevent or minimize any difficult moods or anxiety.

Movement practice can help you identify those symptoms that alert you to a pending mood change if you haven't identified them already. As you exercise, take note of where you feel tension or discomfort or pain. Notice areas that tingle with pleasure or tickle. Experience these sensations in light of your moods and recognize what mental states accompany the varying sensations in your body. If a knot in the shoulder always seems to precede agitation, or if tight calves accompany melancholy, take note. You can discover these things by journaling your experiences, jotting down the quality of your workout and the moods that follow. Patterns will appear and patterns will repeat. Aware of them, you'll be able to intervene to prevent or minimize a difficult episode when patterns that alert you persist.

In the section on meditation I wrote about what forms these interventions may take. An intervention may be as simple as more, or less, exercise; closer attention to the quality of your diet; an avoidance of intoxicants; just enough sleep—don't stay up too late and when the alarm rings spring to and start your day (it's beneficial to go to bed and get up at the same time each day); conversations with people close to you or a therapist who may help you; a PRN, or take-as-needed medication, that your doctor prescribed for just this moment. The key is to work these interventions out in advance with your supporters and caregivers and implement the plan when conditions warrant it. Movement can make you aware of when you need help. Be sure to reach out for this help and take it.

A Fighting Chance

As an example of a surprising practice to which a person can bring their full attention to movement to the exclusion of distractions, consider boxing. It is a complete, present experience.

This may be a surprise, as you may expect meditative movement to be loving and full of peace. Well, it isn't. It's full of what the world serves you right now and how your mind and body react and respond in all their complexity. It can be a flow state or it can be a battle. And to the fighter in the ring, who's to say boxing is not an act of love and peace?

Few who train to box ever make it into the ring, and many of those who do only spar with no intent to injure. It's a great workout. The training is so full of focus right up to the inevitable point that if you don't fully focus you get hit. The sport is athletic and fits the needs of anyone who finds many movement activities full of distractions and self-aggrandizement. Boxing is humbling, and an excellent practice in sustained focused attention, or moving meditation.

Boxing, like many sports, is an art. The only way to improve and realize your full potential in it, as in any movement art, is through dedication and repetition. This is where the focus comes in. This is where the benefit to predicting, preventing and managing episodes of mental illness enters. Dedication and repetition. In jumping rope or hitting a speed bag, a person can bring their complete attention to the act. When the attention wanders a mistake is made and the boxer must start over. Such intense body focus provides the boxer with the chance to silence the doubts of defeat and judgment that pollute a troubled mind. When in tune with the body and its potential, the mind realizes those doubts and judgments are wrong. The body, in fact, over time eventually does what the mind says it can't. It just takes practice. This is liberating and can help to bust through the grip mental illness holds on our sense of self and free us as we realize that our self includes our full body, and our body is just fine, and malleable enough to get even better at everything it does. Why shouldn't our minds be the same?

This is how something like boxing, or football or archery, can pull us beyond the misconception of violence and into the liberating field of enlightenment. The truest threats are not physical and not external, they're the repeated defeatist messages we tell ourselves. Engaging in sports can help us slay those enemies, each of them a demon created by a mind bent on self-destruction. Mental illness wants to tear us down. Through the learning and understanding of movement practice, be it boxing or gymnastics, curling or baseball, we can solidify any foundation of self we may have, even a crumbling, broken one, and build a resilient, confident self on top of it. All of this can come through moving with purpose.

Memory

I don't remember much. There are vast plains of time in my life without a tree or hill or ruined structure on it to force any recall of events or people. I ride into these plains and I'm lost right away; lost in a world wide open, where everything can be seen, but nothing appears. My imagination falters, and fragments of history scatter by, windblown. Every once in a while I catch one and I can see the past.

Mental illness can make your life a living hell and then cover up the evidence with refuse so thick you forget the pain and the havoc that raged. But memories lurk deep within your unconscious. Mental illness can make you forget. This is not uncommon in people predisposed to mania and strikes people with major depression as well.

In the UK a longitudinal study has followed over 9,000 people born in 1958.[9] Researchers periodically measure the health of the people in the study, and of course some of the subjects have grown up to be people with affective disorders. Measures of affect were taken at the ages of 23 and 50. At that point all were tested for cognitive decline. The people with affective disorders have relatively poor memories, and the more frequently mood episodes rumble through their lives, the worse their long-term memory functions. Some of this memory loss is attributed to the neurological effects of misfiring brains, and some to the side effects of treatment.

So how can you hold on to the memories you wish to keep? The researchers recommended spending significant amounts of time with friends and family telling stories, meditation and, maybe most important, exercise.

People who exercise 30 minutes a day retain cognitive function at a higher rate than people who are sedentary. We've already established that this exercise does not have to include trips to grunting gyms, despite what I just wrote about boxing, or expensive classes with people who seem dressed and made up for the Academy Ball. Movement practice can be simpler, and simpler still as one ages.

Walking alone provides almost all of the benefits of more vigorous exercise. Swimming as well. Add some weight-bearing exercise and everything in this section of this book is available to you. It's a miracle that if we purposefully move our bodies and get our heart rates up, even just a little, our brain function, including our memory, will improve. You move with the serious purpose to manage a mental illness. Still, be sure to keep it joyful. Joy is the centerpiece of culture, and we can experience this joy through play.

Chapter Eight

Play

As a kid I never really got into a movement culture. I swam and developed a pretty good backstroke, but movement, this infrequent movement, was not a part of how I defined myself. I remember even then being attracted to the whole skateboarder culture, and when he was out I took my brother's board and risked the slope of our driveway. The board had "Willie Mays, the Say Hey Kid" painted on it, along with a picture of the Giant. It was black and orange and its wheels rattled across every crack in the sidewalk. I was always a little afraid of it, though, and it never became much a part of my life.

The 1970s were all about running. My public middle school had no organized sports, so I joined the St Rose cross-country team. On the first day of practice the coach sent us out to run for what seemed like miles and, exhausted and pained, I ended up crying on a pay phone begging my dad to come pick me up. He told me to finish what I started and hung up. I limped back to the school.

I played soccer my freshman year of high school, but that was it for sports. I despised gym class, huffing the mile and flogging around on the pommel horse, and I made a point to take health class instead of gym during semesters when exercise seemed too taxing. I had no movement in my life and my mind came to a halt. I just hung out on the corner with some other guys and did nothing. Mental illness forced its way into me just then. I'm not saying it wouldn't have happened if I was more fit or active, but most people with mental illness live sedentary lives. I do think I would have handled life better if I was consumed with the discipline, concentration and physical exertion of a solid movement practice.

As an adult I found my first true movement practice in martial arts. I tried everything from boxing to aikido, but found true purpose and full spirit in kendo, Japanese fencing. Kendo, like judo, is a unique combination of movement-as-meditation practice and outright, keep-the-score sport that other arts seek to be but don't quite attain. It brings the full body and mind together in careful motions practiced for centuries. I only realized this, though, because of my teacher, a man named Phuong at a dojo called Koryo in Richmond, Virginia. He embodied the ethos of centered strength and nonviolence through controlled combat that moved me at a time when I was being very violent toward myself.

I was in my late twenties and symptoms of mania and depression were hitting me hard. Kendo practice, especially the drills and forms, was truly moving meditation, a kind of contemplative action. It got to the point that the time I was practicing was the only time I felt sane. In the seemingly frantic world of fighting I held it together. But I couldn't practice all the time and psychotic mania overtook me. I ended up in a psych hospital.

When I was discharged nothing was the same except for the kendo. I couldn't hold a job, I left a relationship, I wasted much of my money. But I'd learned a way of moving and practicing that added focus and soul to the cacophonous pointlessness of my life. I credit that to the wisdom and strength of my teacher.

A good coach is integral to completing the full learning of movement. As children we run for the joy of it, and many adults still do, but with age and experience comes skill, and it is best to learn that skill from someone who first learned it themselves. Trial and error will always be a part of any practice. In the end your point of focus will be your own effort. But every activity, from tennis to skiing, benefits from a lesson or two, or more.

The people to learn from learned from someone else, and there exists lineage. Of course someone was first. Someone first squared off against another in ancient Japan; someone first threw a board onto a wave and hopped on; someone first jumped over a wall in a Paris suburb; everyone in any movement culture can trace their history and their training back to the founder. But even the founders had influences, so there is no discernable beginning to movement. No static state where all was still. A teacher can give you a push in the right direction. A teacher can help you join the generations of practitioners who each brought something full to the art, or activity, or sport. Remember that supervised exercise leads to the improvement of mood as well as medication does. Whether a coach in sport, a master in meditation, or a mentor at work, a guide can help. I spent too much time trying to learn on my own, thinking I was capable and knew better. Manic grandiosity may have been the culprit. My best learning, like at Koryo with Phuong, came through interactions with a teacher. Exercise is simple, and you can work out simple skills on your own. Complicated movement can require assistance.

Even though a teacher can guide you and regulate your technique, never lose your sense of play.

Good Fail!

Movement helps us get out of our heads and into our bodies. Nothing can do this as freely or with such liberation as the sheer joy of play. Play, like nothing else, can improve a bad mood.

I took my daughter to the dilapidated old pier behind the Coast Guard station to run parkour, a free-moving activity of running the shortest distance between two points, even if that means scaling or jumping over obstacles. We climbed stairs that went nowhere; jumped from one broken bench to another; leapt onto and off of a huge tree, burned out by vandals, lying on its side amid the rubble. We skipped stones on the Delaware River. All our worries, the inability to find an agent for me, the drama with the neighborhood girls for her, fell away. As we moved through a dystopian set of what the entire riverfront may look like if the water rises, our minds focused on the challenge of getting from here to there. Over, around or under anything that blocked our path.

And I remembered.

I remembered the big hill in the park with the little creek at the bottom. The path down it along which we kids flew our bikes only to kick hard on the brake and ditch before crashing into the creek. Then came Evel Knievel flying on his motorcycle over a line of trucks on *Wide World of Sports*. We built a ramp. We discovered none of us had the guts to challenge the ramp and attempt to jump to the other side. None of us but one kid. He spun the pedals and hit the ramp and launched so high we had to look up and squint into the sun to see him. He crashed on the other side, valiant and victorious. He did it again and again until he stuck the landing and raced away. These memories of a bicycle flying flashed through my mind as I feebly chased my daughter over walls and along the water. I hadn't thought of that stuff in years.

We were playing, and nothing else mattered. We focused entirely on the moment with each jump, lest we fall. This is the point of movement, and it works best if the activity you choose is playful and even involves a bit of friendly competition.

I admire the cultures of surfers, skateboarders, climbers, martial artists not too enamored of belts, and parkour traceurs. They contain a push to do more, to take their task a little beyond their skill level and improve, all the while settled into the safety of an inclusive group intent on play. An individual may not be accepted right away. One may have to prove oneself with effort. But different personalities with different abilities come together to practice and to play.

Play is a key to mental health. Historically, children have had very low rates of mental illness. The age of onset of affective disorders was accepted to be late adolescence or early adulthood, when responsibility begins to loom large and the playfulness and learning of childhood is replaced by serious efforts to accomplish something measurable, be it in school or in a job. Relationships become more serious and more complicated, and little time is left to let loose and enjoy pointless activity.

Today, children are being diagnosed with mental illness at increasing rates and youth suicide is a real problem, even for tweens, with the rate for boys aged 10 to 14 up 7.2% and girls aged 10 to 14 up 12.7% per year since 2007.[10] What's different? Kids don't freely play anymore, especially physical play. No, video games don't count. They're sedentary activities. Play that is good for the soul involves moving around with abandon and laughing with joy. Overscheduled kids whose every activity is organized and planned don't play. They perform for a purpose. They set out to win because everything they do seems to be overshadowed by some adult keeping score.

Living in the city in a neighborhood with lots of kids, I get to see my daughter play kick the can or wall ball. All ages come together, and competition is intense but fun among friends. They often don't even keep score. Yet even here the kids get whisked away to fierce stuff. Basketball or gymnastics where coaches task 10-year-olds with winning. With nearly everything they do being measured and criticized, it's no wonder kids are breaking. They're not playing. Their focus when they move is on some imposed judgment, not on the beauty of their own bodies.

What does this have to do with adults struggling to manage a mental illness? A lot. People of all ages need to play. Not only are kids not playing, but the parents shuttling the kids around to organized activities aren't playing with their kids. Or with each other. We're frozen into purpose with 24-hour connectivity and endless choices that draw us outside of ourselves and reinforce fear of the unknown instead of enhancing our development. Play is crucial to mental health, and play with movement is the best play of all.

Which brings me back to the surfers, skaters and traceurs. They're not afraid of trying new things, going further, and completely screwing up. There's risk involved. Practice is focused on breaking each move down into its component parts. The focus is intense. Diligent practice done with joy is what this kind of play is all about. We learn, but it's fun. We grow, but that's not the point we seek. What we seek is experience. These alternative-culture athletes seek to master this mindset as they express themselves with their bodies.

At the parkour gym where my daughter trains there is an emphasis on positive failure, for we only learn through failure. This is the silver lining of mental illness—how much growth and learning are possible when we fail. Mental illness is full of failure. So are meditative activities, as we attempt to keep our attention on our body as our attention is constantly pulled away by thoughts or distant sounds. We can incrementally get better. This repeated practice, peppered by setbacks, opens doors to help us be more complete. When an athlete fails at the parkour gym the others congratulate them. "Good fail!" Then on to what can be done differently on the next attempt. In this same way we determine what physical symptoms come before each episode of anxiety, depression or mania. It's trial and error. Every mistake is an opportunity to get better.

In play these attempts and failures are not criticized. They're expected. In play skills are tried and learned, all in a positive atmosphere with little expectation of anything other than a good time. Camaraderie comes whether you're casting flies or bowling in a league. Movement brings people together and is crucial to a healthy body and healthy mind. That's why it helps to keep any efforts toward physical fitness playful. Avoid the drone and grind of the same workout every day and avoid the constant measurement of too much drive toward competition. We all know those hyper-competitive people who are no fun to be around. It's not about how many reps you did. It's that you did them at all. You improved a little and brightened your mood and spirit while doing them.

Play will inevitably lead to competition. The alternative-culture athletes I admire so much will goad themselves and one another on to greater challenges and greater achievement, all the while pushing and testing limits in the name of camaraderie. My experience with these athletes reveals that the best competition is born of community. It's friendly, positive and cooperative. Tricks and techniques are shared and the least able are brought along to improve just as much as the most gifted. As much movement artists as movement athletes, these individuals pursuing individual gains coalesce into a culture bent on standing apart from and getting better than the mainstream. Play and competition align to create movement. Movement in a playful way allows us to bring great focus to our efforts. All of this can help us move toward an experience in which the body and mind are fully integrated.

Join Others

If you can, bring yourself to play in a group or on a team. Just as meditation benefits from community, so does movement. We are not animals hunting solo. Humans have always done their best work in packs. An individual may set up the game, surely someone will stand out as the star, but the support of a group is necessary to truly move from one place to another. So it is with play and sport. Even games played by individuals are enhanced by a bit of competition with others.

Competing with a group can be fun and it can present an opportunity to join something larger than yourself. You're less likely to skip a game when others depend on you than you are to stay in bed on a cold, rainy morning even though the night before you promised yourself you'd get up early and jog. To join something life affirming and heart rate stirring can be a tremendous step toward mental health. In reviewing the benefits of movement practice, team sports have the strongest positive effect on mood.

People tend to automatically project the narrative of the past into the future. Someone who is out of shape and without motivation will naturally see themselves as being that way next week, next month, next year and beyond. Participating in sports, exercising with a bit of competition, is one way to overcome this continuous projection of a negative view of oneself.

Sport, from a friendly round of golf to a pick-up basketball game, enables a person to feel part of something larger than their misery and to observe themselves as active with evidence of improvement. Instead of dreading tomorrow as more of the same, one can look forward to tomorrow as an opportunity to compete and do something physical. Then tell stories about it. These stories, whether the friendly verbal sparring after a game is decided or a personal review of events with a sense of accomplishment or a decision to try harder next time, can change that internal narrative of defeat into one of acceptance and promise. You don't even have to be good at your sport. You just have to get out, try your best, and spend some time with others.

In this way even movement can contribute to a sense of community and inclusion and counter the feelings of alienation and malaise that are so common in those of us with mental illness.

Even more benefit comes to you when you move outdoors. It's indisputable that time spent in nature can benefit mental health in countless ways—from stress relief to a feeling of being connected with something spiritual. I live in the city, so natural space is limited. There are parks, and even tree-lined streets, so I walk through them as often as I can. My family and I take trips out of the city to the beach or the woods, or to farms to pick strawberries or pumpkins, whenever possible, and although I often resist the outing, when I get into nature I always find a sense of peace and presence that escapes me in the city.

Movement outdoors puts us in touch with something primal and natural that can never be obtained in a crowded gym with music blaring and your every move reflected in a mirror. Just as many people try meditation and soon quit, many people make resolutions to get in shape, join a gym, and barely last a couple of weeks. Forget the expense and the fancy clothes and expensive sneakers. You don't need them. Movement is an activity you do all day, not just at a gym or in a class. Don't view it as something to check off a list and then get on with other things. Movement is key to your physical and mental health. It's hard to be out of shape and fully overcome the challenges of an affective disorder. To be stagnant is to rot without hope. By being in touch with your body and bringing your mind to your full range of motion, you can understand and manage your full range of moods.

There are many ways to move, and often the most basic, the simplest yet elegant, are the most beneficial. Choose any practice that works for you, from the intricate postures of tai chi to the weightless drifting of swimming. To bring your mind and body together as one, as they are meant to be, to focus your attention on movement, can be as uncomplicated as walking.

Chapter Nine

Walking

I've written about movement practices from boxing to parkour, but let's face it, not everyone is up to those activities or even wants to participate in such activities. Age or present level of fitness may restrict people to more moderate exercise. Or one may just want something more introspective, seemingly effortless but just as effective for health as sports or other activities. Maybe one wants to truly create space to meditate while exercising.

I can't say enough good about walking. In a new city or through the same neighborhood I've lived in for years, I sometimes want to just stroll about, see things, meet people. On retreat at many monasteries walking is given as much attention as seated meditation. The health impact of walking is indisputable, both for physical and mental health.

A study of 4,500 people with affective disorders, measured across age groups, found that walking is always related to an improvement in mental health when those who walk are compared to groups who do not exercise at all. Always. In fact, people who walk for 30 minutes 3–5 times a week have a 30% reduced risk of becoming depressed.[11]

The physical effects are just as astounding. So many diseases comorbid with affective disorders, like cardiovascular disease, diabetes, pulmonary disease, musculoskeletal disease and obesity, can be positively impacted by walking. It's about as simple an exercise as you can get, but for the mind it may be one of the most effective. Sure, as with any other movement practice, you can buy special shoes and clothes and apps that track your steps, but you don't have to. You just have to get out and walk. It's really a joy. I even like walking in the rain.

I shoot for 10,000 steps, or about 5 miles per day. This is a lot, but not as much as you think. Just wandering around, from the couch to the refrigerator or out to get the mail, the average person walks 2000 to 3000 steps each day. That's without even trying. Build in a regular walking routine and the extra steps naturally add on. Walking up and down stairs adds even more benefit. A Harvard study showed that men who walk up eight flights per day enjoy a 33% lower mortality rate.[12] Walking, through its effects on mental health, can make you want to stay alive. Through its physical effects it can definitively help keep you alive.

Walking as Meditation

A brisk walk can set the day at ease or fire within you the energy needed to complete a crammed schedule. It can help pull you out of defeatist idle time and bring you back to a more positive frame of mind. I know some people who even take their meetings walking. It tends to break down hierarchy and open people up to a freer exchange of ideas. But there's another way to walk, more deliberate, more intentional. Walking can be a meditation practice unequaled in the availability of parts of the body to focus on to enable you to fully experience the breadth of your feelings and emotions at a very specific point in time.

At Zen monasteries they call it *kinhin*. It's a walk at varying paces that divides periods of *zazen*, or seated meditation. At the charterhouse the Carthusian monks go out for a long walk once a week and it's the only time they get to speak to one another. There's another practice, though. More formal and, frankly, pretty silly looking. You may want to retreat to a private place, indoors or out, to try this. You don't need a lot of space. Just enough room to take about eight to ten normal steps, turn around, and head back the other way. What you'll do is repeat this, back and forth, with honed focus. It's best to be barefoot, but shoes are fine, too.

Stand still and face straight ahead. While you can take this walk at any pace, it's best to keep it very slow so you can break the very simple, taken-for-granted act of walking down into detailed parts. Take a full breath, exhale, and then begin to walk, just a few steps, across your space. Come to rest and just stand and breathe for a moment. When ready, slowly turn around, with deep attention and intent, and as slowly as you can walk back to where you began.

Now you have the basic idea. As you turn and begin to walk again, slowly, bring your full attention into your feet. As you step forward, feel the heel of one foot touch the floor as the foot begins to roll forward onto the ball of the foot. Sense when the opposite foot lifts from the ground and slowly swings forward until its heel sets down. Bring your full attention into this work of the feet touching the floor, moving, and lifting again. Feel the weight of the body shift with each step, as if when a foot lifts the body falls forward until a foot touches down again and catches the fall, keeping you upright. There's freedom in that falling and, when the opposite foot swings forward to catch you and save the body from stumbling, security. Continue until you come to the end of your path, then slowly, deliberately with great focus, turn around. Feel the shifting weight of the body and the adjustment the body makes to retain balance during this gentle half-spin. Take a moment, and then begin walking again, and then turn around, and then back again. Back and forth, over and over. Slowly.

As with any meditation practice your mind will wander. When you notice it, bring the attention back into the feet or the feelings in your legs. If the hands feel awkward and you don't know what to do with them just clasp them together or gently fold one over the other and hold them lightly against your abdomen. Feel the calves tighten, the upper legs flex. Feel the miracle of walking. Stay with this for several minutes. Keep bringing your attention back to the act of walking when your mind wanders, and fully experience how difficult this simple act we've never paid attention to is. It's a miracle a baby ever even gets up onto their feet.

I remember when our daughter was an infant. We watched her struggle to stand upright, leaning against objects, pulling at her weight. She'd let go, wobble, and fall. Then she'd turn right back to it. Standing on her own wasn't enough, so she undertook the herculean effort required just to take a step. Eventually she pulled it all together and learned how to walk. We helped her for a while, holding her hands, but soon she didn't want that help at all and wanted to be free to walk where she chose. Those first steps are our first expression of independence. Those first steps illustrate the mind and body working as one. In walking meditation we can regain that sense of wonder—that sense of self-sufficiency. We can be like infants again, fully present, fully focused, concerned with only our own mobility and what the body needs to do next.

That concern has limits. When we walk we just walk. If we think about it too much and try to foresee the next physical act, the whole exercise falls apart. It seems so easy and automatic until we start paying too much attention to it. Walking meditation allows us to be fully focused on the effort but not anticipate what comes next. It, like all good meditation, is training to fully notice what is going on right now, to the exclusion of all irrelevant information that distracts us.

What we need to investigate are the sensations in our bodies that do distract us. In these we will find the most revealing signs that will allow us to predict stirring episodes of anxiety, depression or mania. As in seated meditation, use walking as a means to survey the body and experience the physical stressors found in very specific areas of the body. Something as seemingly irrelevant as a dull ache in the ball of the foot or a tingling in the dangling hands may be enough to inform you that a mood change is imminent. This awareness of an emerging mood, this focus on the physical embodiment of that mood, may be enough to temper the severity of any sudden mood swings. Through practice you can predict mood changes. By continuing to practice you can often moderate them.

This is easier said than done. It takes an awful lot of attention to the body to fully fathom the meaning that our physical feelings reveal. You have to pay attention over time and carefully relate how you feel physically to how you feel emotionally. When you're sad what do you feel in your body? When you're exuberant what physical sensations accompany this elation? When you're anxious does your posture or the feelings in your gut change? What else happens? Note, through practice, the relationship between your body and your mind. You'll find that challenging moods come hand in hand with changes in your physical health. Study yourself closely, because these sensations in the body may be subtle. When you draw a connection between a mood and a feeling in the body through practice, you can be sure that, through practice, when you again notice that feeling in the body the mood that accompanies it is imminent. The mind is full of distractions, so you will almost always notice the telling signs in the body first. This knowledge that something is amiss will give you the space to act to prevent or moderate the mind's trend toward anxiety or a bad mood. No matter where your mind takes you, you can always practice in your body and anchor disabling thoughts and emotions so they don't carry you away.

The mind and the body are intimately connected. One will reveal volumes about the other. The language of mental illness is often spoken through our nerves and our muscles and our joints. Listen to this language during movement such as walking. It will tell you exactly what is happening and exactly what you should do to change it. Then keep practicing. The same movements that tell you when an episode is coming can also, if you continue to practice, help diminish any problems in the mind. Your body speaks. Listen to it and act.

Treading back and forth with your attention fixed (of course your mind will constantly wander, just bring it back), feel into all of your body. Scan one body part at a time, but don't lose your balance or your pace. If this is too difficult just keep the attention in your feet and legs. Notice if your pace is quickening. Truly feel the actions of your body. At the end of each group of steps in one direction, as you turn, take a few deeply felt breaths and be aware of your full body. You may feel tightness in your shoulders. Your head may fall forward and your eyes stare at the floor. Breathe and return to an erect but relaxed posture, look ahead, and walk.

After a while you'll likely feel your legs cramp a bit. Pull your attention back into your feet and feel how they flex and roll through each step, all of the muscles of each foot engaged, pulsing on the floor. You'll realize how silly you look. I was at a long retreat and for a couple of days all we did was sit for a half-hour and walk for a half-hour, from 6 a.m. to 9 p.m., with only short breaks for meals. The retreat center was full of aging hippies as staff, and I thought the men with ponytails and tie-dye ridiculous. But at some point I told one I was from the meditation group. He laughed and said, "Oh, the zombie walkers," and I realized that I, in fact, was the one who looked ridiculous. But the practice was transformative and full of insight. You don't have to do it every other half-hour for days, either. Short periods of walking meditation can give you much insight into your body and how it anticipates and experiences anxiety and mood changes. All of this back-and-forth will focus the mind, exhaust your store of erroneous self-judgments, and give you the space to be well and realize when you aren't.

Chapter Ten

Maybe It's the Discipline

It takes great discipline to exercise regularly, especially when struck with the comorbidities, side effects, lethargy or agitation so prevalent in people with anxiety and mood disorders. It takes even greater discipline to practice this movement with great focus, free of distractions, all of one's attention placed on the body, even to the exclusion of a persistent jumble of thoughts. When I exercise I'd rather listen to a podcast or interesting music than move in silence with my mind set firmly in my body. I'll admit I often dismiss the silence and invite such distractions into the time I spend moving. That does little good for me in improving my ability to overcome difficult episodes. I still get the physical benefits of exercise, but many of the mental ones slip away.

The power of these practices in focused attention are the natural and tested benefits they provide the practitioner. While consistent efforts to bring the full attention onto some point of focus, like the body during movement, will actually change both the cortical structure and the biochemistry of the brain for good, to get the full utility of these practices you have to keep doing them. Some of the pluses stop if you stop, so they have to become an integral part of your day to day in order to have the full positive impact on your lifestyle. The promises made in this book are obtainable, but you have to do the work. This requires tremendous discipline.

When the word "discipline" is used today, thoughts immediately jump to punishment. It has a negative connotation. It's something we do to our kids to correct bad behavior. Discipline also means a system or code of behavior implemented to meet some standard of conduct. That is where I place the emphasis.

Discipline supports both the development of reasonable goals and the practices to implement to achieve those goals. Goals and discipline go hand in hand. It makes sense to have a plan; something toward which you aspire. For the purpose of this book that goal can be to live successfully with a mental illness. Your personal definition of success begins the process. Determine what you want out of life, develop some steps to get you there, and detail your plan. Then adhere to the discipline required to meet each milepost along the way. Measure and merit your progress. Pursue each goal with the tenacity required to succeed. This requires great discipline. Discipline in its most positive sense.

Working toward a goal is scary, especially after being held back in a prison of inconsistency established by your experience with an affective disorder. I took little steps to overcome this fear. First I began writing. Even writing, moving the muscles of the hand guiding the pen across the page, can be a movement practice. I submitted a few articles to websites I read and then launched my own blog. For a while everything was rejected and my blog received very few hits. This was exactly what I feared. I could have quit right then. I stuck to it. Setbacks are an energy suck, so I determined the time of day I had the most energy and disciplined myself to arrange my life so I could muster all that I had, sit, and write right then. I continued to submit articles and my writing improved, based on some fearful criticism I received and, eventually, listened to. Eventually editors accepted some of my pieces. My blog became more popular. Disciplined effort helped me overcome my fears and do the work required to approach my goals and end up in a place of success. It's the same with all movement practice.

As I wrote earlier, once we are diagnosed with a mental illness we have an excuse for everything. This excuse is so often used that failure becomes expected of us and self-discipline becomes rare. We can regain a sense of self-discipline in many ways. A regular movement practice is one such way.

Exercising every day, applying self-discipline to stick to a goal and a task, works as therapy to increase impulse control. This can really help when mood changes seduce us into bad behavior. There was a time when I was tempted to stay out all night and engage in some very risky behavior. All sorts of illicit pleasures beckoned and my life began to come apart. I missed work, I lost friends, I spent more money than I had. I began to run.

It was as if I was running from something, but I couldn't tell exactly what. Instead of sitting idle trying to figure it out, I'd get up early, lace up and head to a path through a large park with small hills. Soon the nights became impossible. If I was going to keep running and get in shape I had to stay in at night and go to bed. It was a struggle, but that's what I did. Soon whatever it was I was running from transformed into something I was running toward. What I was running toward was a better life. My moods improved and my behavior improved. The possibilities open to me improved. Life is all about possibility. We need something we believe is available for us to go on. Good health is possible. Good health creates more opportunities in life. More becomes possible. Movement did that for me.

Impulse Control

While the results of a practice in focused attention like movement are well-researched, the neurological mechanisms involved are indeterminate. This practice does in fact change your brain. Exactly why this happens is not yet known, but it does happen. It could be the attention itself or the release of self-defeating thoughts. Or, it could be the discipline.

Of the people I teach, the only ones who become serious about practice and see true improvement in their lives are the ones who set aside a regular time each day and commit to practice.

For them, it becomes a part of their lives, and soon the day just seems wrong if they do not practice. People who don't establish this discipline quickly fall away from practice and the benefits it can yield. Just as meditation requires the relentless return of attention to a point of focus as the mind wanders, movement requires equal discipline to begin and maintain a practice with body awareness and to make it a greater part of a person's life.

Inherent in many people with serious mental illness is a lack of impulse control. We often follow the trappings of our minds into dangerous and defeated places. We often act with reactivity without awareness of the impact of our actions. We are encouraged in this behavior by a culture that makes every want immediately available, whether we're ready for it or not; whether we can pay for it or not. And boy, sometimes do we pay. To introduce self-discipline into the allure of immediate gratification is difficult. We can view it as stunting and boring. Or we can see it as an opportunity to regroup and draw on our greatest strengths to achieve the things of which we are most capable.

I began a movement practice years ago, and while the stress relief and relaxation benefits appeared almost immediately, the true work of changing my mind took months. I had to get up every day and work out. This was difficult because I had a very low opinion of myself and no motivation, which the exercise soon corrected, and although I had all the time in the world I convinced myself I didn't have time for this. In practice, each moment is an opportunity to return to the present truth, disregard erroneous thoughts and, one day perhaps, develop an impartial awareness of our own mind. All of this can be gained from exercising with focus. Only with such practice can the certainty that we are not captives to our impulses, and that we don't have to act on our impulses, be revealed.

This takes great discipline, but then, so do most accomplishments. I know several very successful people and every one of them worked with tremendous sacrifice and intent to achieve the things they've done. Things for themselves, their families and others. They work on their minds and they work on their health. I believe that for many of them the daily practice of disciplined effort becomes as important as the development of other work habits and sensible choices—perhaps even more important.

Doing something difficult but beneficial every day will likely yield positive results. Little will come to the person not willing to do the work. The discipline of movement is worth it. It can change your life and lead to better mental health as the discipline to practice leads to self-control when moods change, and to better decisions when impulses tempt you.

Perseverance and Purpose

Science has verified what meditation, movement and meaningful work can do for a misfiring brain. Focused attention is held up as one of the most effective things one can do to help predict, prevent and manage the episodes and challenges that interrupt the life of everyone with an affective disorder. Sometimes, however, I think the real benefit comes merely from the discipline it takes to practice consistently.

The effort to stick with something, no matter what or how hard, is essential to develop character and fortitude. The feeling "I can't" must be replaced by the action "I'll try" if any progress is to be made toward the strength required for good mental health. I'm not advocating for replacing defeatist language with positive affirmations. I'm saying that we who seek to live well despite our diagnoses have to have the perseverance and purpose to get up and do what is required, whether it's a good day or a bad day.

You can develop these traits with movement practice. Start with a little bit several days a week. Build up from there.

It's not what you think about yourself that signifies your

ability to go on, it's your capability to do what is required, to maintain the effort even when it seems pointless. Often that needling voice inside of you will whisper, "Don't bother. It's not worth it." Only self-discipline will help you battle this propensity to quit and replace it with a burning necessity to achieve something. Even if that something is as simple and seemingly insignificant as bringing your full attention into your body while you bang out a few push-ups or take a short walk.

Movement practice, exercise, is free. When you feel the residual effects of the work after you move, you'll receive immediate feedback that you have done something positive. Even if it hurts a little the next day. Don't overdo it, but don't lay off, either. Place your attention in your body when you move. Feel the responses and reactions of your entire self to the act of moving, from your head to your feet. Study yourself as you would a challenging subject in school. With this practice those physical warning signs that signal an onset of anxiety, depression or mania will be revealed for you to recognize and respond to. The beauty of movement practice is that the same practice you use to realize the episode may be the intervention needed to overcome the episode. What is revelatory is also the cure.

Discipline is at the root of all effort, even practices in focused attention. In your life you have to move. You should make the most of it.

Section Three

Meaningful Work

To live well is to work well, to show a good activity.
—Thomas Aquinas, 1225–74

Chapter Eleven

The Necessity of Work

Freud said: "Love and work are the cornerstones of our humanness." Productivity, getting things done, is key to feeling alive, having good mental health, and developing the sense of responsibility that enables us to connect with others. It also goes a long way toward combatting the alienation felt by so many with mental illness. Work can be a tremendous way to express oneself. Undertaken with focus, discipline and the love that Freud correlates with it, work can even be used as a vehicle to both improve wellness and predict disruptive mood changes. When it comes to living successfully with an affective disorder, meaningful work becomes the most important therapy of all.

Can any work be meaningful or is that too much to ask? There are plenty of mind-numbing, repetitive, poorly paying jobs, and often that's the work that people with severe mental illness find themselves doing, if they can work in competitive employment at all. I've been there. After years spent moving up in a financial services company, I made it. I ran the sales force. The work engaged me and I loved it. Then the full force of bipolar disorder struck me and I lost it all. I spent the next two years jumping from one menial job to another. I filed papers, I tagged prices on tableware, I made coffee. But I had this sense that I had to keep working. So I did, and it became the practice that set me up for recovery. For a while.

I got back into finance in the money-stuffed buzz of the stock market in the late 1990s. I traded stocks. I rode the high as the market exploded for anyone with a few dollars to spare and a dart to throw at the financial pages. Everyone made a killing. But it all ended and with a violent mood change I fell back to earth, just like the market. Mania took me, and after a couple of hospitalizations and a long course of electro-convulsive therapy I moved back in with my parents, pawned most of what I owned, and rode the bus into Philadelphia to sit at a desk and make cold calls to sell tickets and subscriptions to the orchestra.

But I kept working.

It went on like this until I started meditating. Then I made work my meditation. There was a short time on disability, and another job making coffee.

But I kept working.

The time I spent on disability nearly did me in. I lay listless in the house and thought only of ways to kill time, and then rejected every good idea and just continued to do nothing. I studied a bit, which kept me focused, but I still put in the mandatory waiting period and applied for Social Security Disability Income (SSDI). My claim was rejected, and it was the best thing that ever happened to me. I needed money. I needed medical insurance. I needed to get off food stamps.

I kept working.

There's something magical about getting up every day and adding something, even a little something, to the world. Something that wasn't there before. For a while it was espresso drinks for people at a coffee shop. Then it was a new set of strings strung on an old guitar for $10 a pack at a music store. Then it was numbers in cells on a spreadsheet in an accounting department. All work that many would describe as unfulfilling, boring, meaningless even.

But I kept working. And I healed.

One of the cruelest things that happens to those of us with mental illness is that people stop expecting things of us. They expect us to let them down. Their low expectations define us as dependent, ill, without bearing or motivation. They just assume we can't be fully responsible for ourselves. Usually, we deliver. We accept the low expectations of people, often the people who know us best, the people who should know better, and we give them just what they expect. Little to nothing.

The ugliest part of this stigma is this: That we can't get out of our own way or contribute to our own employ; that we need to be taken care of. Well, we do need other people and we do, sometimes, need help. But we need them to set a bar that we can, that we have to, reach and clear on our own. Then we need those people to get out of the way. We must have the opportunity to encounter and overcome mishaps, not avoid them, by ourselves.

If we give in to, or even worse, if we embody this stigma of low expectations, there is no way we'll find independence. We'll only invite the derision, unintentional as it often is, that we are too sick to fully encounter the stresses and rewards of work. We'll be denied, of our own volition, the joy of a life well-lived.

Our families and others close to us may hold us tightly and sincerely want to prevent us from suffering. Not expecting much of people with mental illness can be the result of love— love intended to keep us from harm. If episodes of anxiety, depression or mania are triggered by stress events, those who love us will of course work to keep us away from all stressors. But the well-meaning, forgivable actions to protect us from one kind of stress result in other forms of stress, the stressors of dependency and poor outlook, piling on. A person has to be productive. A person has to be given the opportunity to take care of themselves. A person has to fail every once in a while. A person has to fall down. And get back up.

Accept the low expectations of society, of family, and invite failure. Or worse, stagnation. Failure is OK if you learn from it. You can get back up on your feet no matter what knocks you down. Increase your expectations of yourself and strive to set yourself up to get better and work. But like meditation and movement, work takes effort and focus. It's a simple idea, but very complicated to implement. And very necessary to put aside any stigma against us and overcome the low expectations that hold us down and keep us there. Our families will be proud of us, and society will welcome us. Encourage us, even.

Approach Tasks with an Open Mind

The work hasn't always been fulfilling. I worked at a retail store that sold shaving cream and razors. I'd ride the 57 bus with my daughter, drop her off at daycare, then walk back to Market Street to catch the 17 or 33 into Center City. Much of the day was spent staring out of the window at the harried people hurrying by along Walnut Street, most of them, almost all of them, completely disinterested in what we had to sell. The days could drag on for insufferable hours.

Then there were the people. The shop had two barbers, and another guy on the floor, and we traded stories. It was easy to stand in awe of this varied but common experience as we expressed ourselves, and every day we laughed. Camaraderie can make up for mind-numbing work, and in time spent with co-workers and/or customers even unskilled work can become meaningful.

My daughter brought a fresh perspective. She loved to come into the shop, eat peppermints we kept in a drawer, stand on a box behind the counter and scan barcodes. Just the beep of the scan gun made her giggle. To a beginner, everything is a new challenge. Try to maintain that wonder. Capture that spirit always and you can learn as much from a cash register as you can from a poem. Any task approached with an open mind can help you grow and keep you well.

Pay is another thing entirely, and such jobs usually don't pay very much or last very long. There is nothing romantic in not getting by. There is nothing rewarding in working all day but having to skip lunch. It's still better to pass the hours with work rather than idle, and better to contribute in any way possible to your own survival. Work beats assistance anytime, and only through work can you get ahead and make things better. Don't suffer indignity, not from the people who pay you, be they your boss or the state. Be active, lobby hard, work for justice and be sure your voice is heard. Change jobs when you have to, if one is available. If not, hold on to what you have while you constantly look for something better. Study, learn, prepare. Don't settle. Keep working. Be prepared to pause when you need to, but don't quit. Through work you can make things better out of life and its responsibilities. Just sitting idle, everything decays.

In advocating for work, almost any work, I may come across as a tool for a system and a culture that contributes, through the depersonalization and devaluation of work, to the high levels of mental illness we have today. While the organization of society may be a precipitating factor in mood disorders, and social injustices may prejudice and exacerbate people's psychological difficulties, that's not a set of ideas that I choose to delve into. I'm concerned with being productive and independent. The ability to bring your full focus to an activity must be developed. If you want to change the world, that's a prerequisite. If you're fine with the world just as it is, you'll find it a lot more rewarding to express yourself through work and to contribute to your own well-being and the health and success of those around you. Work can do much of this as it teaches you, as well.

Work and knowledge are the results of action. It's not what you know, it's what you do that counts. I'm not saying suspend your intellect, and I certainly don't want to imply that work without meaning is rewarding work. But any job is a start. From any place of effort you can enter a life of progress and growth. Take a task and do it well, for the good comes not from what you know, but what you do. Life is a path and it requires activity.

Of course, one of the most tremendous activities is to learn, but even in accumulating knowledge the reward comes in the study and the gradual enlightenment more than in sitting back and saying, "OK. Now I know something." Life is a series of tasks, and through those tasks, through our work, we discover ourselves and the ways we impact others. Through those activities we can measure our moods and judge the present state of our health. Self-discipline and self-awareness are forged in effort, and the process precedes any completion. When we make something, be it a cabinet, a meal or a new mathematical formula, we develop through the work. The finished product is for others. The work itself serves to improve us.

One of the things I liked about growing up Catholic was the emphasis on one's works, rather than declaration of faith or personal relationship with God, as the true path to salvation. The Word was all about one's inclusion in, and influence on, community. I remember in catechism class being taught the prescriptive that it is better to teach a person to fish than to give them a fish, and this injunction toward pulling one's own weight stuck.

The same tradition that emphasizes the need to support oneself and help others through work realizes that society is not always arranged to help people like those of us with mental illness find adequate and suitable work. As Pope Saint John Paul II said: "The obligation to earn one's bread by the sweat of one's brow also presumes the right to do so. A society in which this right is systemically denied, in which economic policies do not allow workers to reach satisfactory levels of employment, cannot be justified."

We ran into this during the Covid-19 pandemic. People and companies failed through no fault of their own, and society was called together to provide more than meager assistance and to facilitate every unemployed person's return to work. The shutdown illustrated the foundational necessity of work to each individual, especially as work shifted from one set of tasks performed each day to unforeseen others. Many were deemed essential workers, but everyone discovered that to make it through the day or maintain mental health, all work is essential. No one invited the harsh deprivation so many faced during and after the pandemic. Society is properly judged by its response to each person's need for work, both as sustenance and maintenance of health and a healthy sense of self.

A person can't always pull their own weight. I had times when I was so ill that I depended entirely upon others. Short-term disability payments and a room at my parents' house were what kept me off the street during my most psychotic mania. Just as community must be arranged to offer work to those who are able, it must gently serve those who cannot work at this time. For some, as it was for me, it may only be for a time. Then the person can heal, relearn and return to work, able again to pay it forward and help others.

When things don't go the way we planned, or the way we would have liked them to go, work can pull us out of an episode that seizes us and place us back on stable ground. It's important to get out and stay active and just do something, especially something with others, when our moods threaten to overwhelm us and drive us inside, alone. Measure the thoughts that conspire to convince you to quit. Make good, reasonable, unemotional decisions about taking time off. I try to save my sick days for when I come down with something other people can catch. I know that deep in the grips of a bad episode I feel like I can infect everyone with my negativity. There is nothing blacker than a dark mood, and during one we can feel our negativity pull the shades and darken the room where every crowd gathers with us in it. Often our mere presence, our ability to merely try, can lighten that space. By toughing it out and going to work, by applying whatever effort we can muster toward making things and doing things for others, we can get better. Give yourself permission to fail in this. But give yourself permission to try. Ignore the voice within you that says, "Why bother?" Ignore the voice that says you're worthless. Any period of contemplation will reveal these thoughts as false. Actually, you're worth a lot. So is your work.

I'm not saying you should shut up, put your head down, and

go to work regardless of what's going on, or that your ability to heal rests on your ability to just tough it out during rough times. I'm not saying your self-worth depends entirely on your work. If you truly need a break, take one. If you can't cope alone, get help. Don't sit out every difficult patch, but don't crack under pressure you shouldn't be bearing by yourself, either. Know your limits. Early in my career I drove on despite what my mind and body told me. I thought it was just a physical struggle. I thought I had to win. I ended up in a psych hospital for three weeks.

Life's all about balance, and nothing will throw you off balance like the mood swings of an affective disorder. You can do a lot to strike a healthy balance between ambition and caution, but it won't always hold. That's why I focus so strongly on developing the skill of predicting difficult episodes. Once you feel one coming you must intervene. You must take whatever steps are necessary to remain stable. These could be medical, or you could just require a break. Yes, you must work, but you must work on yourself, too. If the drive to achieve or the pressures of a job are taking you to unhealthy places, you must take a break and reassess. We're not always up to what we think we are. Persevere, but respect your limits.

Don't be timid, but don't crack because you're too rigid, either. Work can be healing, but there are times when the wrong work can hurt. As you apply effort, whether on the job or at a hobby, constantly assess what's going on in your body and your mind. Be aware of what it is that you are doing. Stay focused and learn about yourself, the things you act on, the world around you and your work. Work filled with focused attention can offer all the benefits of meditation. Of course, if you don't like your situation you can change your body and change your mind, but you just may have to change your situation first. Always respect what your body is telling you. Investigate your thoughts for errors and fallacies, just like you would during meditation. Be honest with yourself and adapt.

Find work that suits you. Forget others' expectations, but don't forget others. You'll need to work with them to truly succeed. Know what you can and can't do. Push through boundaries, but moderately, at least at first. Realize you can take pleasure in and be proud of all the work you do. Through careful focused attention, by turning common everyday tasks like doing the dishes or cleaning a bathroom into meditations, you'll know when to soldier on with more complicated tasks and when to quit. Either at the right time can be appropriate. Always get back to work.

Chapter Twelve

Holy Work and Hobbies

Psychology, especially pop psychology, swings between the ideas that we find ourselves and that we create ourselves. In meaningful work the answer may be found. Whether practicing clarinet or building model ships, diagnosing a disease from a complicated set of symptoms or undertaking forensic accounting, wiring a wall or cutting tile, all good work requires the laborer to bring their full capabilities to the job and, through work, express themselves. In such work people can discover their motivations and their moods. Everyone has the capacity to work, just as everyone with an affective disorder has the capacity to be well. We should not underestimate the connection between the two.

If It Pays It's Nice, but It Doesn't Have To

It's too easy to view work as a necessary evil, yet work is so crucial to our well-being and sense of self. If the goal is to do something that heals, something you feel a strong connection to, then realize that meaningful work is not always paid work. Hobbies and volunteering count, too, and sometimes it's necessary to seek these out to enhance your ability to predict, prevent and manage difficult episodes. Avocations can be rewarding and can demand the sort of focused attention required to manage mental illness. Volunteer work can seal a connection to community and is a great way to re-enter the workforce after a catastrophic experience with an affective disorder seems to remove all hope from one's life. Work can be fulfilling, creative and worthy, even if it offers no wages. In such work you may even better find your soul and purpose. Purpose will help establish positive mental health.

Ask your phone the definition of work. It'll say something like: "Activity involving mental or physical effort done in order to achieve purpose or result." Nothing about money. The work I mean to speak of can be, but is not necessarily, a job. Instead, allow work to be something you do that brings meaning to your life.

This sort of work can take all sorts of forms, but it insists we lose the equation of work as drudgery. My youngest uncle, the first in the family to go to college, tells the story of the night of his graduation. Grandpa sat him at the kitchen table and said, "Don't expect to like your job." This could have been soul crushing had Grandpa said, "Don't expect to like what you do." But he didn't say that. He didn't mean that at all. A great tinkerer, gardener and craftsman, Grandpa hated his job. But in a much broader sense, taking in all he spent his time doing, he loved his work.

Countless self-help books advise us to do what we love. This is not always possible with our nine-to-five. Demands like family, health insurance, medicine and countless others force us into jobs that may not be ideal. At best we should hope to be employed at the work for which we're most qualified that pays us what we are worth. But there is other work. Avocations, or hobbies, can fill our time with joy and fulfillment. The best work touches others in positive ways. The best work feeds and frees our souls. We can find this work in many places.

Even if mental illness prevents a person from holding steady, consistent employment, they can still find productive efforts to perform. Things they can proudly point to and say, "Look, I did that." While working in a bank, delivering pizza or fighting as a corporate attorney may not fill one with purpose, maybe time serving at a food bank might; or growing basil and making pesto; or refinishing furniture to sell at a flea market. All work is holy work. And all legal, ethical work is good work.

After a year during which I was hospitalized twice, I was on disability. I tried to go to school to become a nurse, but my head collapsed with the math of chemistry and my mood darkened again. I had for years played classical guitar, so I threw myself at the instrument with abandon. This I could do. I got pretty good, practicing two or three hours a day. I played at a couple art gallery openings. Then I got a job in a guitar shop and proved to myself that I could show up every day and do what was required. Just like that, I was off disability and working toward independence.

It all started with a hobby.

Confidence and work ethic re-established, and symptoms in check largely through the focus and discipline of the work I was doing on the guitar, I moved on to a job in human services and my life jumped and improved. It was harrowing at first. There was the risk of coming off of disability. Short-term disability is one thing. It's available in many places for anyone forced into a pause by ill health, and people return from it to work all the time. But long-term disability can be a trap in which people get caught, tangled in legal nets, scarred by low expectations of families and doctors, and sealed off in a sort of prison of dependence.

Only 12% of those with severe mental illness participate in full-time competitive employment, and few people who receive long-term disability for an affective disorder ever re-enter the workforce.[13] Certainly, some who stay on SSDI need permanent assistance. But many who could work and receive the positive benefits of employment languish trapped on the dole. There is a way off, but it is fraught with fear. Fears include losing healthcare coverage and the risk of what may happen if a job doesn't work out. It's not always possible to immediately return to benefits if a job doesn't work out. The system is set up to keep people from becoming independent. That's why it makes sense to establish a track record of regular work through volunteer service, education or a serious hobby first. You need to know that you can succeed before you re-enter competitive employment.

You need meaningful work. Something that you do with your entire being. Something in which your effort results in a completion of which you can be proud.

Body Work

At monasteries much work is done in support of the monks' time in prayer. Some monasteries make beer, others cheese or wool. All products that call for intense focused labor and, when sold, support the monastery financially. In the Benedictine tradition work is holy. And true holy work is physical labor. In such work we can bring our entire body into the act of creation.

Physical labor doesn't have to be heavy labor. Any task that brings the body into the effort of the mind in order to create something qualifies. When I studied guitar I started with notes on a page that I could read, but the only way to turn that score into music was to physically labor over the fretboard and across the strings. The effort of playing a musical instrument, like the effort of welding pipes, qualifies as physical work. An actor moves on stage. A gardener digs in the dirt. As with any worthy labor, something is created. Something beautiful and new, even if it's been played or built or performed or grown countless times before. The work belongs to the laborers and they share it with others. Or they choose to keep it to themselves. The practice, the concentration, the effort is in the making.

In this way, through effort consistently applied, we cultivate ourselves. We carefully and completely carry out each task and reap the rewards. The rewards may seem very small, but it's all a question of mindset. Too many people with mental illness do little or nothing productive. Yet everyone can accomplish a lot. Start with the laundry. Sweep the floor when it needs it. Give your pet a bath. You can get up and begin to positively impact your world and yourself.

The idea of cultivating yourself can be developed into silly metaphors about gardening, but even growing something in a pot of dirt can be therapy. I bordered the patio with pots of boxwoods, grapevines and spruce, and created a spot that is now my favorite in the entire city. Birds come and the sun reflects brilliant green off the leaves. I can sit out there for hours reading, writing or meditating, taking in all the sounds that surround my little space and let me know that like the entire city I am alive.

This self-cultivation readily comes from writing, too, and sometimes writing begins with something copied. Earlier I told of Lectio Divina and described how reading a significant work can become a contemplative practice. The same monks who read this way also copied manuscripts. By carefully copying meaningful words they gave new birth to the writing. They made it physical. In this work they grew into a deeper understanding of spirit, limitations and potential.

Get a beautiful notebook and a special pen. Sit at a desk in your room or a library. Or a table in a noisy coffee shop or the café in the supermarket. Anywhere you can relax, focus and minimize or deal with distractions. Pull out a work of true spirit: the Bible, a translation of *Shobogenzo*, poems from the Beats, or song lyrics. Anything that moves you. Anything you aspire to. Then begin to copy. Physically form each word with your hand and your pen. Turn this work into a meditation. Live in the ink and the paper of inspiration. Listen to your thoughts and your body and learn.

Or you can use this time for original thought. Journal your day and your dreams. Write poems of lament or essays of joy. Create, work, express yourself. Be open and honest. Don't worry if it's any good. No one has to see it. Or maybe someone should, if you so choose. Such work can be private or public. Each has its own rewards.

If you do journal, make it full of you. Give yourself a

reference to look back on and measure your moods. Be detailed. Look out for patterns of thought that may signal your mood is changing. Just write, and read what you write for signs of confusion or trouble. I mentioned keeping meditation and movement journals. After each period of practice itemize your thoughts and the feelings in your body. Track this against a chart of your moods. Patterns will emerge. Patterns that will enable you to accurately measure your mental health. Patterns that will indicate when you should intervene to head off an episode. Work can make you well. Work like this can let you know when you're not. Express yourself creatively through what you do. Cultivate awareness and focus your attention on effort, pain and joy. The hardest thing about work is beginning. Once underway you can, for a while, become what you do, all the while understanding that all of this making is making you. You can assemble a self that is productive and self-sufficient. You can become through your work. You can discover and experience. You can then set yourself up to work with, and for, others. You can share and serve.

Holy Work

Work in which a person creates something, or improves something, or manipulates the environment for good can be edifying. This is what has long been thought of as holy work. New worlds large and small have sprung from our hands. We express ourselves as we carve out our own piece of the world, call it our own and act on it as artisans. When we make things it is obvious how we serve the divine, and in doing the best work possible, in bringing our full self and spirit to the task, we don't need miracles or signs, or substitutes for life, to establish ourselves as whole. We just act with the tools we make.

Very few people have done this sort of work for a very long time. When monastic rules for work were written, all work was physical labor, and such labor is still assigned on retreat today.

When Dorothy Sayers wrote of the redemptive power of work in the 1940s, most people still worked with their hands. Even though much work was done in factories with machines, laborers still made tangible things, if only a small portion of a larger set. Today most people work in service or in the transmission of information. The theology of work that focuses on task and physical effort seems less easy to apply, if it's applicable at all. We can compensate for this with hobbies. We can make things and in that make ourselves.

In making ourselves through work, we learn, but not all work is conducive to this sort of learning.

People in the trades often have work that is up to the task, and jobs in kitchens, factories, healthcare and the military can be so honored as well. Others may have to replicate the focus required to assemble things and work on detailed, tangible problems in other aspects of their lives, like hobbies.

The options are endless. From cabinet making to martial arts to discrete mathematics, countless avocations can help a person work on focus and discovery. I had a telescope when I was a kid, and lugging it around, setting it up in a dark, open field, and targeting it at a point of light that in the eyepiece turned into an upside-down, colorful image of Saturn or Mars was truly joyful. The focus of trial and error required to bring that distant light into the viewfinder to reveal the sky's secrets was intense. I could spend hours scanning the sky and capturing the heavens. All else fell away. It was just me and all I had in me turning and positioning the scope while the sky cleared and my eyes adjusted to the dark so punctuated by the stars and planets in the sky. Years later I picked up an old scope second-hand and climbed to the roof to take in the few sights available in the never-dark city sky. That old sense of discovery and hours of focus returned, and I truly felt as tuned in to my thoughts and emotions as I was to the craters on the moon.

The focus of the mind and senses on this work is obvious,

but the slow, bending dancing about the tripod made the work physical as well. So tuned in to the task, I was aware of the playing of my mind and stretching of my body during this time spent alone working on just one thing. My father found the same liberty with a metal detector on the beach, and a friend who dances illustrates the full immersion of body and mind in singular effort. They both can easily measure their moods by how the task feels.

As with movement, this type of work should be done in silence. Then, even something as mundane as making dinner can become reflective, holy work. I sauté onions and garlic with only the sound of the oil and the vegetables crackling in the pan and the pungent smells filling the kitchen. No music, no talk, no distractions. I've got nothing against music or talk. All sorts of sounds and rhythms can shape your moods. I just like to work in silence with focus. Work becomes a sacred space. While working I'll notice when the signals that warn me that an episode is imminent interrupt my focus and interrupt my work.

Avocations or side-gigs can supply the tasks that become both meditative and fulfilling. We must not view this work as an escape from real life or an escape from employment. Work that we hold as having little value certainly takes on crucial importance in helping to measure our moods and emotions. Mental health requires a psyche engaged, and hobbies can engage us in ways our paid work may not. Attention focused on what we're doing, every moment we do it, with an equal awareness of the people for whom we do it, is the foundation of ethics, progress and faith. When broken by mental illness, work can fully form us once again. Yet in work and life, in managing difficult moods and living successfully with an affective disorder, we must be prepared to fail.

Failure

Sometimes it seems I can't do anything right, sometimes my

mistakes bowl over any feelings of accomplishment, and sometimes work doesn't help at all. I write of therapies that enable one to prevent, predict and manage the worst of affective disorders, and they work, but sometimes the mental illness wins.

I've lost jobs I've done well and squandered opportunities that should have come easy. I've thrown everything into some new interest that fully engaged me, only to quit later and curse myself for wasted time. While I followed the discipline of work to great success, I've failed in the shifting winds of whim. With these failures I've judged myself harshly. I've thought myself a failure.

Who hasn't? Who hasn't doubted? Doubt is necessary to truly learn. In the old saw: great doubt, great knowledge; little doubt, little knowledge; no doubt, no knowledge. Who has learned anything without failing first? If I do a task right the first time, I learn nothing new. But if I struggle with it, falter, then figure it out, I grow with new knowledge and earned success.

We learn to work. We learn to be well. In that learning we fail until we finally get it right.

I don't brag that I've mastered bipolar disorder, because I haven't. I manage it. Meaningful work helps me, and I couldn't manage without it. Sometimes I am pained to keep my expectations high. Even with steady work, even with dedicated practice, episodes of anxiety, depression and mania still come. They just seem to come less frequently and with much less severity when I'm fully engaged in practice and my life is inspired by good work.

I don't mean for this book to make what I've done, and what I encourage you to do, seem easy. It's not. Hard work is good work, and rewards usually only follow sacrifice. Effort must be made to determine what is truly important and what is worth sticking with through failure—what ideals and goals you'll cling to, what people you'll pray to keep—no matter what. These things to work toward when all is well and to keep in sight when battered by failure make life worth living. It's said nothing good is easy. Mental health meets this limitation. Failure emphasizes all limitations. Work can be the tool we need to measure and overcome such failure and feel the full force of our potential and our possibilities. Also, a reasonable approach to our own failures will make us more forgiving of the failures of others. In failure we find hope. In failure we can discover possibility. We're a work in progress, and when we fall apart, when we fail, work can put us back together again.

Chapter Thirteen

Work as Therapy

At monasteries where Zen and Benedictine monks reside, and many laypeople take retreats, work is a key part of the practice. It seems every time I visit one I'm sent off by the work master to clean bathrooms. At one, as the people on retreat gathered for work assignments, the work master asked if anyone was good in the kitchen. I am, so I raised my hand. He pointed at me and said, "Men's bathroom." As I cursed under my breath I came to realize that work, too, can be a kind of ritual. And it can be a key form of therapy. The stereotypical person with mental illness lies on the couch, remote in hand, afraid to go out lest they jeopardize their disability insurance. This characterization, as well as this sort of lifestyle, traps an individual in a cycle of dependency and despondency, unable to support themselves, unable to reap the positive benefits of work. One of the key benefits of work is the ability to shape and be secure with oneself. Discovery is possible through applied effort. So is the capacity to know when things are just off and an episode of anxiety, depression or mania may be imminent.

It all comes down to paying attention. It's necessary to focus on the task at hand and still take inventory of the thoughts that clutter your mind and the feelings that course through your body — to identify if stress is altering your moods or causing you discomfort. Think about why one day just feels different from another. When you just don't want to do something, exactly what are you feeling in your shoulders and your gut? When these feelings repeat, is the mood attached to them the same? If not, how is it different? How do your thoughts emphasize that difference, or reinforce any similarities?

It's a lot, and just like in meditation rambling thoughts can take your mind off your work. In making work a practice, in determining its impact on your moods, making the effort to remain focused is important. As thoughts distract you from your task, don't chase them or begin an internal conversation. Let each thought go and return to your work. Be a witness to your own experience. As a witness does, make an informed observation about your state of mind.

This will require you to continue to assess, and reassess, what's going on within you. If you are aware of your experience, you can be aware of your moods. Each day may seem different, but try to determine what certain days share in common in your body and in your mind. Truly, what are you feeling and thinking? When patterns reappear, does a particular mood follow? How about areas of tightness, nagging or even relaxation in your body? What do they indicate? What is your body telling you? Observe how others respond to you. Identify your inconsistencies. Understand where you stand in relationship to your steady, healthy state.

Prepare to be surprised. Your moods will not always match your thoughts. In fact, your thoughts may pull you very far away from your task at hand and convince you that you are in an emotional place very far from your reality. Always look out for inconsistencies and those little lies your mind will foist on you. Go deep within with your focus. Your body may tell you more than your mind. I'll state it again, it's like an intense course of study. The subject is yourself. The goal is to know when your moods are changing. The result is to know when to intervene to prevent yourself from getting carried away by a bad situation.

To achieve this level of awareness it is necessary to apply some of the same attention-placing methods used in meditation. This requires either rote, repetitive, often physical work to which you can bring intense focus, or something creative through which you can express, and identify, your changing moods. Your job may not allow for either. You can still perform this type of work through a side-gig or a hobby. It doesn't have to be the sort of work you do for hours on end. Small chunks of time, 20 minutes to a half-hour, are enough to bring your full attention to a task, and to fully experience what's going on in your body and your mind.

Work of Art

A close friend of mine is an artist. Before he paints he spends hours preparing the surface. He builds a frame, attaches a metal sheet to the frame, sands the metal, affixes the proper paper to the metal sheet. With his hands he assures himself that the surface is ready for paint. Imperfections on the surface are part of the work. Before he can begin to paint, though, he must consider color. He must mix the pigments to achieve the effect he seeks, knowing from experience that what he sees on the brush will not dry exactly the same hue. He chooses the proper brush. Only then is he ready to do what most of us would call painting. The entire process, to the artist, is what it takes to paint. The entire process is painting. Brush on paper is only a small part of the effort, and only a fraction of the finished work.

For my friend the finished work is not the purpose but the manifestation of the focused effort, combined with years of experience, that went into what the observer sees when they look at the art. Only a rare viewer sees the action, the task making, that goes into a painting hanging on the wall. For the artist, for my friend, though, the task, the experience, not necessarily the finished painting, is the representation of his effort. While when we look at a painting we see colors and shapes that combine to move us emotionally, for my friend the emotion, the movement, is in the physical effort of making a painting. The work supersedes even the product. To do it is the achievement. When the work is done and hung to be observed, the work, the effort and joy of work, has already passed. So he goes back to work again. In a way, the finished product is incidental. The acts that make up work tell him all he needs to know.

It's no wonder we call it a work of art. It's no wonder we use that phrase, "work of art," to refer to the product of our best effort. Also, we must never lose sight of the word "work" as a verb. While it doesn't define us, it can accomplish us as we do it. To work is to live.

Work, like meditation, can be used as a means of focusing the attention, and as with meditation work can focus the attention on feelings and thoughts that may signal the onset of an episode of anxiety, depression or mania. But first we must break it all down into parts.

Words of Work

I use three words—"work," "task," and "act"—seemingly interchangeably. They're not, so let me define my terms:

- Work is the continued exertion or activity directed to some purpose or end; an occupation or an avocation.
- A task is a specific amount of labor or study required by duty or necessity. You accomplish work by carrying out tasks.
- To act is to attend to a purpose or function; to behave in the moment in a way suitable to complete a task.
- "To act" is the verb required to perform a task. Work is the completion of that effort, or the result of a series of acts taken and tasks completed.

To think of work as therapy requires the practice of bringing focused attention onto each and every act. For when working on tasks, the attention is placed with intent on each act involved in completing each task. The difference between attention and mind-wandering is the difference between acting and not acting with focus. Attention and thinking are not the same thing. If you're thinking about something, that doesn't mean you're paying attention to it. Of course, you can pay attention to something and not think about it. That's the point of some meditation and movement practice. It can apply to work as well. Therapeutic work requires that one attend to each act with complete focus and not get lost in distracting thoughts. When work is broken down into tasks and even further into acts, the feasibility of this sort of focus becomes understandable. Work that lends itself to such focus becomes meaningful.

To break work down into such constituent parts while getting through a busy day begs the question, "Is attention a luxury or a gift?" Obviously, when we truly pay attention to another person it's a gift. But is the ability to attend to work with focus a luxury?

I remember when I was working full time and going to school full time at the same time. There was no time for fancy practices in focused attention or movement other than basic exercise. Many days there wasn't time for that, either. I had no opportunity to focus on anything other than study and work. It seemed attention was a luxury. I hadn't yet learned to bring my full attention to my work. Work, at this point in my life, could not be considered therapy. Instead, it was a burden.

I remember when my daughter was an infant. It seemed every single time she slept and I sat to meditate, no matter what time of day or night, she would cry. I should have sat in the rocker with her and her bottle and brought my full focus to the act of a father feeding an infant, breathing, connected in a timeless way in a darkened room, the very definition of meaning. Unfortunately, I still thought seated meditation was the only practice for focusing on and predicting episodes that needed further attention. It took a while to shake this and learn about true focus through acts. I thought at first, *Damn, she interrupted my meditation again! Can't I get any peace?* I missed the most peaceful moment a parent can grasp. Too many people who advocate meditation think and promote the idea that only deep focus on the breath counts for true practice. They're wrong. There is too much emphasis placed on only that one form of practice. In time, I came around to a more expansive way of viewing practice. I came around to work.

I was teaching a meditation class, and in the class was a father of five kids. I asked him about attention. He said the first child is the most challenging because everything about life changes. You're no longer living for yourself and you can no longer put yourself and what you want to do first. The second child was just a minor adjustment. The third child required a complete shift in attention. He had to reposition from playing man to man to playing zone, and kids just dashed in and out of his cognizance. But he was always aware of them. After that, playbook established, more kids just meant less room. As he placed his attention on the children that swarmed through his awareness, as each act of parenting was attended to, he found true focus, and fatherhood, possible.

Attention is work and, like any work, some of us do it better than others. If we can bring attention to each task, we can practice in ways more profound than the seeming loss of temporality and dismissal of connection to full experience that some mistakenly believe meditation should be.

I think some people get Zen wrong, and some get union with the divine wrong, as if they are merely meditation and prayer and not the practice of life. Zen has a real aesthetic, an expression spoken through manipulated objects—gardens, tea ceremonies, haiku. The craft is in working upon them and the objects' or words' positions. One of the most profound Zen books I have read is called *Sakuteiki*, and it's about gardening. True practice is in the production, the manufacture, the work, the constant inquiry, not just in the meditating in the zendo. Life is a work in progress, and to progress, whether spiritually or to manage a mental illness, or both, we must bring our full attention to the acts that make up our work. Meditation is not sitting down doing nothing. It, like work, is an exploration of effort.

I think Christians on the path make a similar mistake. Life is a cycle, and prayer is the bond that holds one's effort, not something that one does when work is finished. Of course the focus of the Gospels is on the three years Christ taught. We overlook the nearly 30 years he spent working at a job, just like everybody else. Before he was the Messiah he was a laboring carpenter. Grace isn't in the moment of divine union. It's in completing tasks, getting things done for ourselves and, especially, for others. We touch the sacred through our work. It's the key to touching those with whom we share life. It's the key, too, to touching ourselves, to measure and manage our moods. Don't think work is drudgery. It's therapy, and without it we drift away from the light that illuminates our self and enables us to see where we are and where we don't have to be.

Reactions and Responses

Mental illness hijacks our attention. A mood disorder corrupts the way we feel and respond, even about the smallest challenges. These disruptive moods steal our attention and force our focus onto thoughts that conspire to convince us that we are not up to the work, reason and decisions required to live a life within the boundaries of sanity. Not a life of control, because unexpected events will always knock us off the trail we seek to blaze. Relationships, jobs, pandemics and protests will present themselves as obstacles against or opportunities toward our goals. It's at these times that we can feel overwhelmed and become prey to the attention-devouring moods of anxiety, depression or mania. It's not promising to try to control these moods. We have medicine, therapy and the practices in this book to help with that. But even 20 years into the experience of being able to predict, prevent and manage these moods, they still stalk me from time to time and wrestle away my attention from where I choose to place it, and then deposit every thought I have behind walls of worry, fear, aggression or impulse.

This inability to bring focus to my work redirects my carefully calculated responses to events as they occur. Instead, I react without reason. This usually upsets me or someone close to me. In responses, as opposed to reactions, focus allows for good decisions and positive outcomes. Blind reactions to surprising happenings, on the other hand, fuel bad behavior and bad moods.

It's likely that when I'm reactive to things and surprised by my behavior I've lost the capacity to bring my full attention to a task that needs to be done. Coming back to that task, coming back to work, whether that work is on a project or on myself, is the key to accurately surveying my place at the moment and acting, right now, in a way to temper the influence of the vagaries of disruptive moods.

You can't be sure about the outcome of any event, but you can be completely sure about the work that needs to be done now.

We must be careful not to attend too much to the idea of control that constantly eludes us. It's pointless to try to stay in control because everything is always changing, and such a rigid mind set on control can easily break.

I like to talk about attention more than control because "control" is a confusing word. It speaks both of something we do right now and something we try to maintain over time. We clutch it as a goal, failing to distinguish the immediacy of a problem from the horizon toward which we move as we attempt to solve the problem. We never reach the horizon, and we can never be in control for more than a short, poorly defined period.

A better word is to "act." Lots of people advocate that we should live in the moment. I don't know what that means. "Live," like "control," is too broad a word with too long a timeframe to capture right now. To live in the moment is a meaningless directive. However, a person can act in the moment. And to act in a progression of moments is to complete a task.

These acts toward this task, undertaken in the present moment, are what I'm talking about when I'm talking about work. Here work can become therapy. If we're acting in the moment, if we're working, we don't have to wait for things to get better. We're doing better all along. We're acting moment by moment and we're bringing our full attention, in the moment, to our work.

When a mood disrupts our life and we become dismayed at a loss of control, we can still take action right now to push ourselves toward health. By placing our focus on the acts we perform in each moment, instead of allowing it to wander aimlessly, we can free ourselves of the pointless myth of control and actually, positively, influence our own behavior. In the worst of my mixed episodes my mind swirled agitated and dark. It settled on an outcome of surrender to impulse. Usually those impulses were very dangerous. Then I learned to act in the moment. I learned to peel away the layers of despair and do something right now to bring my attention to this very moment. It may have been something as simple as taking a shower (actually, if you've been in this state you know how seemingly impossible even a shower can be). It may have been to call a friend. It may have been to start a project. But I acted. In this action I could pull my attention back from the violent indeterminacy of the life in which I felt trapped and just do something, one thing with focus, and feel productive, capable and touched with purpose through this simple act and the focus I brought to it.

Things can get difficult when the task to act upon encounters impulse. Impulse followed can bring about some of the best moments in life. Think of a first kiss. But impulse can be dangerous, too, and to act on a dangerous impulse can be very costly. To act demands a decision and clarity of thought.

Sometimes this needs to be done very quickly. Work is not only tasks performed over time toward some productive end. It is also carried out in each action in each moment. Each act has repercussions. To bring our full focus onto our acts in the moment can free us of the distracting thoughts that can cloud our vision of these repercussions. I attempted suicide in a very impulsive act, with no knowing premeditation. My life at the time was completely without focus, and without work, and I followed my moods into all sorts of bad behavior. I didn't contemplate the gravity of my actions and I never considered the consequences of my impulses. I was not acting attentively in the moment. I had no practice. I just did, and I did badly.

What separates a life of blind reaction to impulse from a life of reasonable responses is the moment of focus on the act of the moment—the focus required to delineate between right and wrong. Reason can be trained. It is developed through focus on the tasks at hand and a contemplation, however brief, on the impact of our actions on our well-being and, if that fails our search for meaning, on the well-being of others. To carefully carry out tasks does not have to be boring, but it does have to be guided by some morality, some ethic. Our entire sense of right and wrong can be brought to an instant if we focus on what we seek to do, what actions we need to carry out to do it, and then do them well.

We are the consequence of our works, and our works determine the positive mark we leave on the world. In our work, act by act, task by task, we can lose the sickness of the self in purpose, on purpose.

Chapter Fourteen

Work as Experience

Limits and Creativity

It's a common image on motivational posters: a climber scaling a rock face or a hang glider soaring over cliffs that plunge into the sea below. The caption at the bottom proclaims, "Live Without Limits!" We are meant to be inspired. This is terrible advice. The climber and the glider are acutely aware of their limits, as is anyone who intelligently and skillfully undertakes any activity during which they encounter any risk at all. Every activity, from raising a child to applying for a new job to starting a new medication, entails risk and limits.

I can't be anyone I want to be, and the sooner we all disabuse ourselves of this notion, the better. Morality limits me. Talent limits me. There is nothing wrong with these limits. They are there to guide me. Define limits and achieve real freedom. For to be free is not to live without limits. It is to excel, to express oneself, within necessary, ethical, reasonable boundaries. I'm sure it immediately strikes you as odd that I emphasize limits in a book to help you overcome mental illness, but every successful person is schooled in their craft, works within the bounds of a medium, and creates only that which their body and mind can execute. While we may fear that living with a mental illness defines us and inordinately limits us, there are things we can do that others, even others we assume are gifted and exceptional, can't do.

Limits even allow us to foster creativity. They give us boundaries within which we can measure our success and guideposts within which we can achieve. An enormous amount of creativity is required to live successfully with an affective disorder. It doesn't have to be the kind of limit-expanding creativity that fills concert halls or births new industries, but it does have to be creativity that enables you to consider from different points of view your situation and the way the world treats you. It must be creativity focused on solutions and new ways of doing old things, not creativity that merely identifies and offers up problems, then finds new, defeatist ways to complain about them. When your life is at its most negative, creativity, if only through an unconsidered perspective, can be tremendously positive. You have ideas. Open-minded meditative acts will help you discover, formulate and realize them.

We want to be free of the pain and disruptions of episodes of anxiety, depression or mania, but even this freedom requires certain restrictions. To be free of symptoms of mental illness we must respect the treatment regimens developed with our doctors. We must realistically assess our potential as enabled by our gifts and experience, and our drive. We must be forgiving of the self-doubt and past mistakes that stoke our suffering. No matter how many new ideas we follow in our quest to live better, we must consider the impact of our choices on others, the cost of the correctives we choose, and the time we have to properly implement them. Meditation and movement can be free, take relatively little time, and make us more healthy, stable people of positive influence on others. Work ties all of this together. Work and the freedom made possible, even within limits, just because we do it. Which brings us back to creativity. Even when it's innate it must respect limits and be developed through work. Creativity depends on developing experience through having experiences. It makes life worthwhile. We continue, as Dorothy Sayers said, "for the sake of doing a thing that is well worth doing."

Experience
"Experience" is another one of those difficult words that is both a noun and a verb. The noun and the verb are dependent

on each other. You can't have one without the other. You must experience things with focused attention in order to have a full experience; in order to find work meaningful.

Our self, that indeterminate thing doctors diagnose as sick, as having a mental illness, is simply raw material to be developed not by what we are told, or even what we think, but by what we do. Each experience we have builds on another in order to develop who we are. Thought means little in the development of the self, and thought is only a part of predicting, preventing and managing mood changes. If we act instead on what we experience in our bodies as well as in our minds, we will be successful. If we try to figure it all out first, if we deny the evidence we find in our bodies during practices in deep focus such as meditation, movement and meaningful work, we will never respond in time enough to deal with difficult episodes. Doing, and being fully focused on what we are doing, is key.

In fact, thinking about a mood often prevents us from addressing it. We end up left to wallow in our sorrow or race through grandiosity at the whim of our impulses. Experience is a physical thing, an action, the real evidence of who we are. We experience moods, we experience cures. We find ourselves and best manage our moods in what we actually do to pass our days, not in who we think we are. This is why work is so important.

Return for a moment to the idea that work is a process made up of acts and tasks. The accumulated effort, the striving of actions, develops the quality of the work we do. It also develops our self. Again, I am not speaking of paid employment, although for some people their jobs allow for meditative focus. I speak of experiences on which you can place your attention and embody with your entire being physical and mental effort. Work becomes a subversive act in which we tear down what we think about ourselves and replace it with deeply felt experience. This experience is beyond words. We live in the present through concentrated focus, all the while staying in our bodies instead of lost in thought.

Sitting and thinking won't help you predict an episode of anxiety, depression or mania, and it certainly won't help you overcome it. Doing, having experiences, will. No one can tell you this. You can't figure it out. You will never know yourself through your thoughts, and you certainly won't come to know yourself by being told who you are or what you should do, or even why you should do it. You know yourself through your work. These actions that make up work, this experience, will teach you what precipitates or aggravates difficult moods. Keeping your focus on the present, on your actions, inevitably reveals how to act to deal with difficult moods. Thinking about life is not living at all. Doing things and experiencing life is living.

Cassian states that "a busy man is besieged by a single devil, but an idle one is destroyed by spirits innumerable." Meditation, with its fierce concentration on the present, is certainly not time spent idle. Neither, of course, is movement. Sometimes what is required to keep the demons of inconsistent moods away is simply to stay busy. Not staying distractedly busy in the sense of ignoring your full experience, but staying busy to create and embody work. Or, to put it more simply, staying busy just to do something with focus. Experience, that sense of operating in the moment, of being completely in touch with yourself, awakens us alive. When awake with the stimulation and revelation of work, we are less likely to amble in melancholy or race toward irresponsibility. When active, when we work, we are less likely to be haunted by the inherent phantoms of mental illness. This will obviously happen if our experience is a positive one, but even if our experience is negative, if we pay attention to it, we are learning and working on ourselves and our moods. We can focus on the task at hand to the detriment of the runaway thoughts that pull us toward dangerous places. Just by doing, by experiencing things we do as they are, good or bad, we can avoid the cursed state we seek to banish from our lives. The state of not paying attention to our present experience. The state of being ruled by unexpected and untamed moods; the state of anxiety, depression or mania that terrorizes our mental health. Doing protects us from this, and doing defines us.

I'm not saying, "Fake it 'til you make it." I hate that advice. It can make you resent those you work with who seem to have things easier. It will drive a wedge between you and those who don't have to fake their way through the day. It can make you resent yourself and reinforce any erroneous beliefs that you're not up to the tasks that on other days seem possible. Exploring how you respond to work enables you to fully encounter the feelings and thoughts that settle you, drive you or hold you back. Faking it ignores this experience and pulls you out of your body and your mind in some effort to present a false front that may dangerously set yourself up for the crashing realization that you're not the fake you after all. You'll be much worse, and others will probably see through you anyway. You may as well be yourself and do the work.

I spent years developing an incredible ability to fake being well when I felt most rotten. I'd laugh and flirt and speak with charisma as inside I screamed to no one for help. I was divorced from my experience. I was without focus. This is classic mixed-episode behavior, and it led to a resentment of those who were close to me. Others who, because of my faking, had no idea of my suffering. Of course they offered no help. I was refusing to help myself. Even so, I was surprised by their callousness and grew to hate them for it, unaware that they were innocent. The faking enveloped me. I lied to my family. I even lied to my doctor. Everything was OK until it wasn't. The façade would never hold, all came crashing down, and I ended up in the hospital six times because of it.

I was so caught up in faking it that I had no connection to my experience.

Instead of faking it you must experience the changes and the pain. In this way you will be able to accurately assess your state of mind and make positive adjustments. You'll be able to focus on your work. Reflect on your self-talk and its errors. Realize that in faking it we lose touch with our true experience and get all caught up in thoughts. Our minds fill with lies. Be honest with yourself. Live fully in your body. Feel what you feel honestly and breathe. If you can, keep working, but don't show off to yourself. Cry out to those you most trust. Call a friend or a doctor. Realize fully the definition of mindfulness as where you are now and where you don't have to be. This requires complete honesty and an honest focus on your present experience. Do not try to end an episode by faking wellness. Allow it to end by experiencing your state with complete honesty. Practice healthy ways to confront and adjust your behavior. Do the work. Be real. Your mental illness is. You need to be, too.

Chapter Fifteen

Work as Connection to Others

Martin Luther consoled his friend Melanchthon when his friend suffered from a terrible longing and depression not unlike the one Luther himself had once experienced. Luther spoke to his friend of the need for a vocation to turn away from himself and his inner struggle and toward his neighbors. "Get outside yourself!" was Luther's prescriptive. Only through mixing with and working for others could Melanchthon properly satisfy his longing and heal. He had to lose himself, and then rediscover himself, in work for others.

Such a task turns the emphasis away from inward absorption to acting, to doing as a key part of experience. Both our present experience that defines our lives and the experience we gain as we carry out varied tasks and grow, building on things as we interact with the world. Nothing festers like an over-focus on the deficiencies of the self. Nothing fosters like the community we seek through our work.

The best work offers each worker a sense of connection and attachment not only to those we share our work with but to some greater purpose. This doesn't have to be a profound movement or a groundbreaking organization. Just to be part of something, to join a community moving together in an established direction toward a common goal, is enough. To serve others is the entire point of life and the quickest path toward satisfaction and happiness.

Besides employers, churches and clubs and volunteer organizations can offer such community: leading a youth group or joining a runner's club, playing in a band or hunting with friends, gathering with family. Any activity where people come together for a common purpose will help you "get outside yourself" and find stability and meaning often missing in the lonely suffering of anxiety, bipolar disorder or depression.

This sense of attachment is very different from the attachment that some faith traditions condemn as the root of suffering. Attachment to greed and hate drive a person inside into a dark lonely place, walled in and separated from the best in themselves and others. Attachment to community with a positive purpose is different. It requires you to give of yourself; to establish yourself as a positive actor and influencer on the lives of others who are likely just as needy as you are. Everyone suffers. Everyone seeks community. Too much self-focus is detrimental to your health. Healthy attachment to a cause can improve your chances of overcoming mental illness.

Attachment to an individual can be very different and must be carefully examined. There's no love in the abuse or distrust often found when a person with mental illness tries to fill in their own perceived deficiencies by sublimating their life to the will of another person. The attachment I speak of is to work and a purpose in which one can find oneself. Not a relationship or a group into which a person can lose themselves.

If attachment is devoid of true connection it will result in suffering. Whether that connection is with co-workers, teammates or fellow activists, one should only connect oneself to a worthy cause working toward some positive end, not one that imposes its will on others or seeks to destroy things. We hate too much. Communities that promote hate are damaging. True connection is attractive, and when it's discovered others will freely choose to join with you and your community.

Just as this sense of connection to others can help pull a person out of depression, it can help temper the grandiosity found in mania. Family members, partners and close workmates are likely to notice unhealthy changes in your mood. If one of them takes you aside and asks if you're OK, take that as a key sign that an episode may be brewing. Even when you carefully measure your moods, a family member, friend or co-worker may notice changes before you do. Be thankful for their concern and heed their implicit advice to place into play plans you have made to intervene as an episode begins.

If at all possible, if it doesn't cause damage, keep working. That sense of connection and focus can do wonders as you struggle with anxiety or challenging moods. Don't give in to the slippery emotions that convince you that people doubt, or even dislike you. Unless you really screw up, you're unlikely to damage your connection to others in any meaningful way. If you do really screw up, you'll likely find those closest to you may still be there for you. Be prepared to ask for forgiveness. Be prepared to make amends. By honoring this connection, by continuing to adhere to the path and do your work well, whatever your calling, you are less likely to make mistakes that damage your relationships, your community and yourself.

Finding Connection

I worked in a guitar shop with two men who became lifelong friends. They gave me space and time when I needed it, and they offered help when my bipolar disorder demanded it. When all fell apart, they visited me in the hospital and were there for me when I got out. My family, especially my parents, have always been accepting and generous when I seemed without options and without hope. Today my wife gives me support and places my goals and my work as equal to anything she seeks to accomplish for herself, and we both dedicate our best efforts to raising our daughter. I'm one of the lucky ones. I was interviewed on a podcast and the host asked me what I would say to people who don't have this depth of love and support. My wife noticed I stumbled at this question and couldn't quite answer it.

Connection to others is necessary for a person to connect with themselves. People from broken homes or broken relationships have broken connections that they must replace or repair. People who suffer abuse should not have to suffer alone, and they require supportive connections to escape the abuse. If repairing broken connections is possible, take the first step toward reunifying with family or friends. If that's not possible you can seek connection and community elsewhere. You may want to begin with a positive relationship with a therapist.

Faith, even if you're just curious about a faith, can be a great support. I've yet to hear of a church, synagogue, temple or mosque that slammed the door in the face of someone who showed up and said, "I'm curious about your community."

The shutdown during the coronavirus pandemic taught us all that community can be established virtually. People who share interests can come together online and discover people with whom they can explore things they have in common. While I do believe that for many there will be a backlash against all this virtual communication as we search to reestablish in-person connections, the technology will remain a workable place for introductions. Just be cautious of what you reveal online until you know and trust that the people you're sharing with have your best interests at heart. Avoid groups that come together to oppose things through hate. There are plenty of places to positively express yourself.

Peer groups are fonts of support. Any opportunity to come together with people who struggle against common demons toward common purpose is an opportunity to learn, grow and find a place of security and love. Check out organizations like the Depression and Bipolar Support Alliance and the National Alliance on Mental Illness for references and referrals to groups.

A healthy group to join is one which helps you achieve your goals without too strictly influencing through demands just what those goals should be.

I can never underestimate the opportunity work provides for connection to others. Jobs, hobbies and classes all provide recourse to a revelatory community; one with which you can share experience and face and enjoy the challenges and victories of life.

Addiction

This book is about things an individual can do to help themselves predict, prevent and manage episodes of their own mental illness. It places a heavy burden on self-responsibility. But no individual stands alone. We're all part of society and we all owe our best to society. Meaningful work emphasizes that. Society must order itself to help those who seek to help themselves and to offer care to those who, because of mental illness, or any illness for that matter, are not able to help themselves. This extends even to people whose choices may have gotten themselves into a difficult situation to begin with. It's our duty as a caring people.

I've skirted addiction in this work because I have little experience with it. Yet substance abuse remains one of the great mental health crises of our time. Half of all people with bipolar disorder or depression also have a problem with drugs or alcohol. It serves no one to declare that an addict's addiction is their own damn fault and it's their responsibility to come clean. I know enough to know that's not how addiction works. That's not how compassionate society should work either.

The alienation of addicts and those with mental illness is one of the great tragedies of our culture. We must investigate why so many people feel alienated and abandoned, and what that means for all of us.

I state again that "alienation" is a very old word. Its original meaning was "to be separated from one's God." It's obvious that a person who feels so separate finds no meaning in society and, sometimes, no meaning in themselves. The inverse, too, is true. Society finds no meaning in them. We've sacrificed common good and common purpose to empower each individual with a slew of rights independent of how the exercise of those rights may impact others. Then we've given each person the tools, in the form of alcohol, street drugs and opioids, to do themselves in. We must not rise high and mighty and blame the user for their own demise. Yes, like anyone else the addict must take the responsibility to get better, but overcoming addiction takes more than a choice to do so. It takes structure provided by society to both empower and enable the addict to help themselves.

Outrageously, meaningful work is denied to so many whose addictions have crossed them with the law. When ex-felons are denied the healing and earning of a vocation, how can they get better and successfully re-enter functional society? How can we expect them to?

Practices in attention like meditation, movement and meaningful work can help in the healing of addiction if the addict uses the time to contemplate what positive things the substance added to their lives as they took it. Ellen Langer, a scholar and researcher who approaches mindfulness from a uniquely non-Eastern perspective, posits that only if we determine the good the addict receives from their using can we begin to replace that good with something more wholesome and edifying. Everyone, especially the addict, knows that substance abuse is wrong. But in a blunt way, to the addict it once served some positive purpose. Perhaps through meaningful work that purpose can be uncovered and eventually, with a lot of necessary community help, the substance can be replaced with something healthier.

People abusing drugs or alcohol often feel alienated. We must reel them back in, offer them something to work toward and believe in, offer the connection they seek, in order to correct the assumption that they are alone. Unfortunately, with the decay of so many societal structures and the poor replacement of far-flung technological communities that offer little individual attention or feedback, we reinforce that they are, in fact, alone. Self-care is impossible in a society that couldn't care less. I fear the self-care movement has simply further isolated people from one another, all concerned with their own well-being, while many fail, lost from a connection to people who believe in something greater than themselves — and believe in one another.

It is a corruption of spiritual practices to remain inwardly focused as one grows. For what can one so focused grow into but a selfish, self-important isolation? We end up in an odd place where people who fail feel alienated and, conversely, people who succeed feel like they've done it all on their own, just as alienated from social good as the ones they ignore in their quest for self-improvement and, God forbid, self-actualization.

I believe the ascendant cult of self-worth overall breeds more addiction and, with it, more mental illness. For one thing, those afflicted know, as did our great, now ignored spiritual masters, that self-focus is a poor substitute for service. In serving others in a healthy way, instead of in serving oneself without doubt or recourse, sanity can be found; both the sanity of society and the sanity of the individual. Meaningful work meets this end.

What You Owe to Those Who Help

I've already stated that society should be arranged to help those who through illness or disadvantage cannot keep up with the demands and challenges of regular work. Whether it's for a lifetime or for a short period, disability insurance enables each person to remain a vital part of their community and to contribute in any way they can. Even if it's only toward their own healing. As the world gets larger and once-reliable providers of care like churches, community groups, personal charities and, above all, families splinter and shrink, the agencies that provide such help and care get more distant and less personalized. It's easy to turn on them and feel entitled. It's easy to lose a sense of responsibility to the group.

Even when the assistance check is written by some huge government bureaucracy, we must not lose sight of the individuals who through their taxes and insurance premiums fund this support. Societal support goes both ways. Each of these individuals who fund social programs are making a sacrifice, giving up experiences and things they could have, to provide the money for all social services. When I was on food stamps and disability insurance I felt an incredible connection and responsibility to this faceless but significant group. When I felt like quitting my meds or following some ill-advised impulse, I thought of them. They were helping me, whether they knew it or not. I had a severe responsibility to get better if I could, just to thank them. Then, as I got back on my feet and recovered, I was glad to pay it forward. This is community.

We all should feel this responsibility and this charity. We all should feel personally culpable when the system fails someone, or when someone fails the system. People who are psychotic or debilitated by mental illness should not be expected to play along and buy into a myth of unbending self-reliance. We need other people. We must help. Still, most people with affective disorders are able to understand the sacrifices others make and acknowledge their responsibility to those people who give. This is how we come together and accept one another.

The hope of this book is to help people get well. Wellness is required whether one wants to excel within a system or change the system. Everything can be improved, but we must begin by improving ourselves. Then we can approach a troubled society from an untroubled space. Of course we must create an untroubled space for ourselves first. Meditation, movement and meaningful work, living life with focused attention and clear, honest community-based intent, can help create that space. We all must decide what type of world we want to live in and how we can nudge the world in that direction. I wouldn't have the audacity to tell you what kind of world you must have, but I hope I've given you a method to create the world that best serves you, your loved ones and your community, as small or as large as you choose to define it. It's a tremendous responsibility to become well. It takes work. This kind of work can inspire awe as it creates change. The beautiful fact is that in doing this work, for both personal and community development, we can both sow the seeds for individual healing and cultivate influence that will be felt by others. The prescription and the cure lie in meaningful work. The mere undertaking of positive work on yourself and for others will heal both yourself and your world.

The faith traditions I've appealed to are not paths to individual salvation. The love of the Abrahamic faiths only exists within our interactions with and compassion for others. In Buddhism, in the Pali Canon the eightfold path leads to civic society, not enlightenment of the individual. Every action is political. So are all our views. In working toward wellness and independence we're making the statement that mental illness does not condemn a person to a life of changeless subordination. While goals may sometimes have to be reined in, at least for a while, goals are worth making and goals are attainable. Don't let your mental illness define you. Manage it and live fully.

Conclusion

Always Return to the Body

A person with a mental illness has the unique advantage of the intimate knowledge that as moods change, a person lies underneath the rubble, waiting to emerge into a period of remission or another, different, episode. This person can be found through practices in focused attention that stand separate from the moods that in dysfunction seem to define them.

However, when I'm in the grip of depression or the terror-filled flight of psychotic mania there is nothing else. There is just that mood and the overwhelming sense there always has been, and always will be, the thoughts and feelings that pummel me while I'm in that mood, as if it always has been that way, and always will be that way. I am trapped inside this pall of despair and often it is so real that there simply is nothing else. By coming into contact with the reality of the mind and body, exclusive of the mood or the erroneous stream of thoughts that perpetuates it, I can be liberated from the difficulty. But I have to first focus on the sensations in my body before the thoughts in my mind. I have to pull away from the assault of challenging moods and the thoughts that aggravate them into the truth of the mind and body as one, breathing, moving or working, independent of the stories I tell myself that drive me into episodes of anxiety, depression or mania.

There is a feeling in the body when all is well. Mental health depends on alive alertness, an assurance that all is just so and settled — that rare session of balance in meditation, flow state in movement, or oneness with the task during work. This feeling implies activity, not a stagnant period lost in thoughts of grandiosity or defeat full of repeated stories of the way things were or the way things ought to be. It's a brief taste of not wanting anything else.

This we will never be able to put into words, but we will know, and we will live with the knowledge that through doing, not actively thinking or talking, we can be free of the ever-playing repetition of damage and illness. Suffering is not to be minimized. It is real. It is a nonverbal experience that is caused by the false stories we tell ourselves as we languish in terrible moods. The only remedy is to go to the body. Then we can defeat the pull toward what makes us suffer.

It's telling that in the Bible Yahweh defines His identity as "I am He who is." Just "I am." In the Pali Canon the Buddha describes himself as "I am he who is just so." Just "I am," again. No object, no adjectives. We are the same, and in practice we just are. Mental illness drives us to be something we are not. It disrupts any sense of balance between the body and the mind. It makes us sick.

So what is sick? Our bodies. Inseparable from our mind, restricted by the language we use to describe ourselves, our advantages and our deficiencies, our bodies breathe and move and work no matter what we call ourselves, remember ourselves as, or predict who we will become. If there is illness it must be found there. If there is healing it must be found there. In the body. Always return to the body. There we will find our own base "I am."

The body joins the mind and we are born. Onto the mind and body together we layer moods. Expressed by thoughts a mood is something new. Something separate, something malleable. Something dependent on language. Moods become relational. They rely on what we are thinking and how that compares to other, similar times. Anxiety, depression and mania install their own descriptive words that force us into moods, and mental illness can be the result. Attempts, and successes, to penetrate this language and reside in the mind and body moving as one, whether through the breath or movement or work, can heal this division hoisted on us by the alienating, incendiary and often erroneous stories we tell about ourselves. We must free ourselves from these inaccuracies to truly heal and finally be able to care, for ourselves and for others. Wittgenstein said: "Nothing is as difficult as not deceiving oneself." Through an intense focus on what simply is, the focus we can achieve through meditation, movement and meaningful work, we can free ourselves of this deception.

I return to the idea that mental illness is a disease of the body. It is discovered in the body. It changes the body, and the body, and subsequently the mind, responds to practices in focused attention and physical medical treatment. What if mental illness is entirely an experience of the body? The stories that seem to aggravate it, the self-talk that makes us sick, can be dismissed to allow us to completely confront our illness as a physical experience. To move first with it, and finally free of it. To emerge from the trap of illness we must discover ourselves independent of what we think we know. Thoughts, ideas and stories can change our minds. Diet, exercise and sleep can change our bodies. But we always exist in the present, simply, and in the present we find that we can be OK, free of pretense, not lost in some past that formed us or some future that expects us.

All we have for certain is what is actually happening right now. This is entirely a physical experience. Our thoughts are generated by the physiology of the brain and, if we narrow the present moment, even the thoughts become irrelevant. All we are left with is our body and its senses. This is our full experience. Stories muck this up because they are always changing. They are hard to keep consistent. The human mind hates inconsistency. It is almost irresistibly inclined to harmonize with the body. In meditation, movement and meaningful work we just allow it.

Practice matters. Having a full experience of the mind and the body together is our true state of wellness. When we separate the two because of illness and try to treat only the mind when, in fact, the body too is ill, we end up with mental illness. We apply therapeutic language to diagnose, explain and treat something as nonverbal as cancer or gout. Our attempts to treat mental illness are often too narrow. They focus too heavily on our minds. We must include an investigation of the body and all the body experiences in any investigation of what ails us. If we can bring meditation, movement and meaningful work into each day, reaching for every moment, we may not fully overcome mental illness, but we will be able to predict, prevent and manage difficult episodes. We can discover the truth in our sense of self. We can reconnect with the person under the rubble—who we really are. We can live without, or with a lot less, anxiety, depression and mania.

* * *

I believe mental illness springs from some difficulty in my mind and body, some separation of the two. I believe the practices I've presented can heal this rift. I also believe these practices are very effective for dealing with the difficulties of day-to-day life.

Medication also helps. Therapy, too. While the practices in this book are among the only ways to fully experience the present moment, unify the mind and body, consider the symptoms and warning signs, and accurately predict episodes in this brief instant, I still have the practical questions of how did I get into this mess and how do I get out of it? Here an appeal to talk therapy has its place, for there are things to do in life and things we must resolve. The resolution of trauma and abuse will benefit from the techniques in this book, but introspective consideration through therapy will also greatly help.

This is the twenty-first century and I am pragmatic. I have a wife and we have a daughter. We have to plan for college and retirement. The car needs an oil change and the computer needs to be charged. My daughter needs occasional help with her homework and my parents need rides to doctors' appointments. The methods in this book are very practical and help me with all that. We live in a challenging world. Wisdom developed over time through listening to and noticing the body, through focusing on the present moment, is necessary to function beyond the present moment. In a profound way, a full focus on the present moment through practice adequately prepares us for an honest consideration of the future and can reveal the best ways to act when we move beyond the present into that future. Practice helps us live well.

To me, meditation, movement and meaningful work are essential. They may be for you, too. As I've written, they are not things you do and then go do something else. To survive and flourish with mental illness these practices must be fully lived and fully expressed every day. I need to bring my full attention onto everything I do, whether that's reading the Psalms or making a grocery list. We can all do it. We can all recover. Then we can live better day to day in the world we are given, the world we can shape, this world we have.

No matter where we find ourselves we can be accomplished and charitable, living fully with others in concert with consistent moods. *Practicing Mental Illness* may be a provocative title for a book, but in always practicing, in accepting and improving, we can separate ourselves from the limitations and lamentations of mental illness and live a coherent, moral and rewarding life.

This is real. I've done it. Every day I review where I am right now and where I don't have to be. Every day through practices in focused attention, through practicing mental illness, I can heal and press on into a world in which I belong. Challenges never cease, but we each can develop skills to meet them, measure them, confront them, and thrive.

Appendix

Standing Meditation

From my book *Resilience: Handling Anxiety in a Time of Crisis*

Stand barefoot with your feet shoulder-width apart and let your hands fall naturally to your sides. Pull your shoulders back slightly and don't lock your knees. Keep them soft throughout.

Posture is important, but you don't have to be military formal. Close the eyes if you can, or simply hold the gaze in soft focus at a spot on the floor a few feet in front of you. Keep your head up.

Pull up and gently drop the shoulders two or three times, and take a few deep breaths. Check the knees to see if they have locked, and relax the shoulders.

Stand in silence for a few minutes, first feeling the muscles in the feet constantly adjust, different parts of the sole in contact with the floor at different times as the body keeps its balance. Feel into the calves as the body settles in. Check the knees and shoulders again. The knees may keep locking and the shoulders may keep creeping up toward the ears. Relax. Stand in silence for a few minutes. Really try this. Don't read on until you have. You'll spoil the fun.

I bet you were surprised at how much you move by just standing still. The body moves around a lot, as if the legs are the trunk of a tree and the upper body the branches swaying in the wind. As the body constantly adjusts and rebalances, some people even experience a bit of motion sickness. It's always a surprise to feel this. I've practiced this way countless times and it still impresses me. Apparently, there is no such thing as truly standing still.

Loosen your knees again and reposition your shoulders.

Stand quietly for a few more minutes.

Take a deep breath. Roll your shoulders backwards a few times, and then forward. Stretch your neck slowly, carefully, from side to side, then front to back. Check your knees and shoulders again. Feel your feet, calves and thighs. Take another deep breath, and go ahead and slowly sit down.

People are often astounded to discover how much goes into just standing still. They're struck by all the things they never noticed, especially all the swaying, while doing something they've done all their lives. This shows you the incredible power of discovery and the ability to notice new things when you focus your attention on your body.

If by standing still for a few minutes you can notice things your body does that you've missed your entire life, imagine how you can develop the ability to notice slight or profound changes in your body that may signal an episode of anxiety is imminent.

Just pay attention, and as you practice daily note when things feel different. When things feel odd do any unusual thoughts bubble up? When you focus on an area of tension or discomfort does your mind change? This can be very telling.

At a more basic level, note the things you feel that signal that you're stressed. I find I'll get a knot in my left shoulder and a cramping and popping in my left jaw. My forehead and my brow feel tight. Most alarming is discomfort in the right side of my abdomen. It can actually harden, ball up and sharply hurt.

In just going through the motions from day to day I often notice none of this until it's too late. Before I know it anxiety or some other mood change strikes. But if I practice in my body through movement or standing still, I know when a challenging time is coming. I feel it early. I know what to do. You can develop this skill, too.

About the Author

After a series of hospitalizations and a lot of bad behavior, George Hofmann managed to overcome the worst of bipolar disorder by adding practices in focused attention to the usual therapies of medicine and talk. He works to show others with anxiety, depression and bipolar disorder how to do the same. George can be found at the site "Practicing Mental Illness," which promotes meditation, movement and meaningful work as keys to growth and healing. His book *Resilience: Handling Anxiety in a Time of Crisis* was published by Changemakers in 2020. George writes commentary on the Psalms from an inquisitive, ecumenical perspective at The Psalms Meditations Project. He lives in Philadelphia, Pennsylvania with his wife, their daughter and two poorly behaved dogs.

www.practicingmentalillness.com

Notes

1. Bittman, M, Sipthorp, M (2011), Turned on, tuned in or dropped out? *LSAC Annual Statistical Report 2011*
2. Schlosser, M, Sparby, T et al (2019), Unpleasant meditation-related experiences in regular meditators, *PLOS One*
3. Edelstein, J (2019), Generation Z is finding its Zen, *Civic Science*
4. Goldstein, B, Liu, S et al (2011), The burden of obesity among adults with bipolar disorder in the United States, *Bipolar Disorders*
5. University of Oxford (2014), Many mental illnesses reduce life expectancy more than heavy smoking, *Science Daily*
6. Carta, M, Conti, A et al (2015), The burden of depressive and bipolar disorders in celiac disease, *Clinical Practice and Epidemiology in Mental Health*
7. Chandrasekaran, V, Brennan-Olsen, S et al (2019), Bipolar disorder and bone health: A systematic review, *Journal of Affective Disorders*
8. Hearing, C, Chang, W et al (2016), Physical exercise for treatment of mood disorders: A critical review, *Current Behavioral Neuroscience Reports*
9. Power, C, Elliott, J (2006), Cohort profile: 1958 British birth cohort (National Child Development Survey), *International Journal of Epidemiology*
10. National Institute of Mental Health (2020), Suicide
11. Wein, K (2011) The exercise effect, *American Psychological Association*
12. ibid.
13. Mechanic, D, Bilder, S, McAlpine, D (2002), Employing persons with serious mental illness, *Health Affairs*

CHANGEMAKERS
BOOKS

TRANSFORMATION

Transform your life, transform your world - Changemakers
Books publishes for individuals committed to transforming their
lives and transforming the world. Our readers seek to become
positive, powerful agents of change. Changemakers Books
inform, inspire, and provide practical wisdom and skills to
empower us to write the next chapter of humanity's future.
If you have enjoyed this book, why not tell other readers by
posting a review on your preferred book site.

Recent bestsellers from Changemakers Books are:

Integration
The Power of Being Co-Active in Work and Life
Ann Betz, Karen Kimsey-House
Integration examines how we came to be polarized in our dealing
with self and other, and what we can do to move from an either/
or state to a more effective and fulfilling way of being.
Paperback: 978-1-78279-865-1 ebook: 978-1-78279-866-8

Bleating Hearts
The Hidden World of Animal Suffering
Mark Hawthorne
An investigation of how animals are exploited for
entertainment, apparel, research, military weapons, sport, art,
religion, food, and more.
Paperback: 978-1-78099-851-0 ebook: 978-1-78099-850-3

Lead Yourself First!
Indispensable Lessons in Business and in Life
Michelle Ray
Are you ready to become the leader of your own life? Apply
simple, powerful strategies to take charge of yourself, your
career, your destiny.
Paperback: 978-1-78279-703-6 ebook: 978-1-78279-702-9

Burnout to Brilliance
Strategies for Sustainable Success
Jayne Morris
Routinely running on reserves? This book helps you transform
your life from burnout to brilliance with strategies for sustainable
success.
Paperback: 978-1-78279-439-4 ebook: 978-1-78279-438-7

Goddess Calling
Inspirational Messages & Meditations of Sacred Feminine
Liberation Thealogy
Rev. Dr. Karen Tate
A book of messages and meditations using Goddess archetypes
and mythologies, aimed at educating and inspiring those with
the desire to incorporate a feminine face of God into their
spirituality.
Paperback: 978-1-78279-442-4 ebook: 978-1-78279-441-7

The Master Communicator's Handbook
Teresa Erickson, Tim Ward
Discover how to have the most communicative impact in this
guide by professional communicators with over 30 years of
experience advising leaders of global organizations.
Paperback: 978-1-78535-153-2 ebook: 978-1-78535-154-9

Meditation in the Wild
Buddhism's Origin in the Heart of Nature
Charles S. Fisher Ph.D.
A history of Raw Nature as the Buddha's first teacher, inspiring
some followers to retreat there in search of truth.
Paperback: 978-1-78099-692-9 ebook: 978-1-78099-691-2

Ripening Time
Inside Stories for Aging with Grace
Sherry Ruth Anderson
Ripening Time gives us an indispensable guidebook for growing
into the deep places of wisdom as we age.
Paperback: 978-1-78099-963-0 ebook: 978-1-78099-962-3

Striking at the Roots
A Practical Guide to Animal Activism
Mark Hawthorne
A manual for successful animal activism from an author with
first-hand experience speaking out on behalf of animals.
Paperback: 978-1-84694-091-0 ebook: 978-1-84694-653-0

Readers of ebooks can buy or view any of these bestsellers by
clicking on the live link in the title. Most titles are published
in paperback and as an ebook. Paperbacks are available in
traditional bookshops. Both print and ebook formats are available
online.

Find more titles and sign up to our readers' newsletter at
http://www.johnhuntpublishing.com/transformation
Follow us on Facebook at
https://www.facebook.com/Changemakersbooks